THE CORONATION VOYAGE

THE CORONATION VOYAGE

Michel Marc Bouchard

Translated by
Linda Gaboriau

Talonbooks
1999

Talonbooks
P.O. Box 2076, Vancouver, British Columbia, Canada V6B 3S3
www.talonbooks.com

Typeset in New Baskerville and printed and bound in Canada by
Hignell Printing Ltd.

Second Printing: July 2003

The publisher gratefully acknowledges the financial support of the
Canada Council for the Arts; the Government of Canada through the
Book Publishing Industry Development Program; and the Province
of British Columbia through the British Columbia Arts Council for
our publishing activities.

Le voyage du Couronnement was published in the original French by
Leméac Éditeur, Montréal, Québec in 1995.

Canadian Cataloguing in Publication Data

Bouchard, Michel Marc, 1958-
 [Voyage du couronnement. English]
 The coronation voyage

A play.
Translation of: Le voyage du couronnement.
ISBN 0-88922-422-6

I. Gaboriau, Linda. II. Title.
PS8553.O7745V6913 1999 C842'.54   C99-910806-9
PQ3919.2.B682V6913 1999

Les pieds dans les glaieuls, il dort. Souriant comme
sourirait un enfant malade, il fait un somme:
Nature, berce-le chaudement: il a froid.
Les parfums ne font pas frissoner sa narine;
il dort dans le soleil, la main sur la poitrine tranquille.
Il a deux trous rouges au côté droit.

      —*Dormeur du Val*, Arthur Rimbaud, October 1870.

The father who gave you life destroyed that life.
Your father hands you over to extinction and walks away.

      —*Iphigeneia at Aulis*, Euripides

The playwright would like to thank Captain Jacques Decoster, the passengers and the crew of the *Cast Otter* with whom he shared the transatlantic crossing in May 1990.

Special thanks to Dominique Lafon and Benoît Lagrandeur.

Le voyage du Couronnement was first performed at Salle Pierre-Mercure, Centre Pierre-Péladeau, Montreal, on September 21, 1995, with the following cast:

Rémy Girard	THE CHIEF
Marc Béland	HYACINTHE
Hugolin Chevrette	SANDRO
Monique Leyrac	ALICE GENDRON
Gérard Poirier	MINISTER JOSEPH GENDRON
Robert Lalonde	THE DIPLOMAT
Benoit Gouin	THE BIOGRAPHER
Roxanne Boulianne	MARGUERITE GENDRON
Lorraine Côté	MADEMOISELLE LAVALLÉE
Marie-France Duquette	ÉLISABETH MÉNARD
Manon	ÉLISABETH TURCOTTE
Caroline Stephenson	ÉLISABETH PENNINGTON
Henri Pardo	JEREMY
Matin-David Peters	WILLY

Directed by René-Richard Cyr
Assisted by Geneviève Lagacé
Set Design by Claude Goyette
Costumes by François St-Aubin
Lighting by Denis Guérette
Sound by Robert Caux

This production was co-produced by Théâtre du Nouveau Monde, under the artistic direction of Lorraine Pintal, and by Théâtre du Trident, under the artistic direction of Serge Denoncourt.

The Coronation Voyage was first co-produced by Alberta Theatre Projects, D. Michael Dobbin, Producing Director, as part of *PanCanadian playRites '2K'* (Calgary), and Belfry Theatre (Victoria) and premiered at Alberta Theatre Projects on January 29, 2000, with the following cast:

Peter Millard	THE CHIEF
Lucas Myers	ÉTIENNE
Brendan Hunter	SANDRO
Donna Belleville	ALICE GENDRON
David Adams	MINISTER JOSEPH GENDRON
Todd Waite	THE DIPLOMAT
Tom Rooney	THE BIOGRAPHER
Shannon Anderson	MARGUERITE GENDRON
Heather Lea MacCallum	MADEMOISELLE LAVALLÉE
Tiffany Thomas	ÉLISABETH MÉNARD
Sheila Reader	ÉLISABETH TURCOTTE
Iam Coulter	ÉLISABETH PENNINGTON
Frank Zotter	JEREMY
Shaker Pelaja	WILLY

Directed by Roy Surette
Set design by Judith Bowden
Costumes by David Boechler
Lighting by Brian Pincott
Sound by Allan Rae
Production Dramaturge: Vanessa Porteous

The English translation was first presented in a staged reading directed by Peter Hinton at Interact 96, a showcase event co-produced in Toronto by Factory Theatre and Centre des auteurs dramatiques.

For the benefit of readers who might wish to compare this translation with the original as published by Leméac Éditeur, it is important to note that, at the playwright's request, the translation is based on the script as it was extensively revised for the English-language première co-produced by Alberta Theatre Projects (Calgary) and The Belfry Theatre (Victoria) in January 2000. The translation of the revised version was made possible with the assistance of the 1999 Banff *playRites* Colony—a partnership between the Canada Council for the Arts, The Banff Centre for the Arts, and Alberta Theatre Projects.

The Passengers

The Chief. Mafioso. Father of Étienne and Sandro.

Étienne.* Twenty-five-year-old son of the Chief and Sandro's half-brother.

Sandro. Thirteen-year-old son of the Chief and Étienne's half-brother.

The Biographer. The Chief's biographer.

The Diplomat. Trade Commissioner at the Canadian High Commission in London. World War II veteran.

Marguerite Gendron. Pianist in her early twenties. Daughter of the Minister.

Minister Joseph Gendron. Politician. Liberal Party Minister in the federal government.

Alice Gendron. The Minister's wife.

Mademoiselle Lavallée. Protocol officer.

Élisabeth Turcotte, Élisabeth Ménard, and Élisabeth Pennington. Young women in their twenties who have won a trip to London to attend the Coronation procession.

Jeremy and Willy. Black, English-speaking stewards on the Empress of France.

*The Chief's oldest son was called Hyacinthe in the original French-language version.

Part One

Episode 1

THE BIOGRAPHER:
> Early in the morning, an excited crowd stormed
> aboard the majestic Canadian Pacific oceanliner,
> the Royal Mail Steamship Empress of France. On
> the quay, a military marching band led the farewell
> festivities, adding to the general excitement.
> (*Marching band.*) Shortly before noon, the
> departure signal was sounded for the first time.
> (*Fog horn.*) Passengers stood waving goodbye on
> every deck of the ship. Only the deck reserved for
> first-class passengers was almost deserted. At one
> end, a dapper man carrying a cage with two birds
> strode briskly across the deck. At the other end,
> came Sandro, distracted, a Coca-Cola in his hand.
> The dapper gentleman and the boy collided
> head-on. It was noon. On May 22, 1953.
>
> *THE DIPLOMAT and SANDRO appear on the first-class
> deck. The Diplomat is covered with Coke.*

THE DIPLOMAT:
> What a scatterbrain!

SANDRO:
> I'm a real scatterbrain!

THE DIPLOMAT:
You could have looked where you were going!

SANDRO:
I should have looked where I was going.

THE DIPLOMAT:
This is very unpleasant.

SANDRO:
It must be very unpleasant.

THE DIPLOMAT:
You've ruined my suit.

SANDRO:
I've ruined your suit?

THE DIPLOMAT:
Stop repeating everything I say.

SANDRO:
Immediately, sir.

THE DIPLOMAT:
Don't stand so close to me.

SANDRO:
There's a tailor on board.

THE DIPLOMAT:
Let's forget the whole incident.

SANDRO:
My father will pay.

THE DIPLOMAT:
Don't stand so close to me.

SANDRO:

It's because of my glasses. I should wear them, but my father doesn't like them. He says they make me look ugly.

THE DIPLOMAT:

Young man—

SANDRO:

My father will pay.

THE DIPLOMAT:

Let's forget the whole incident.

SANDRO:

Are those your birds?

THE DIPLOMAT:

They're horned larks.

SANDRO:

Do you take them everywhere with you?

THE DIPLOMAT:

They're a present from the Canadian diplomatic service to the London Zoo on the occasion of the Coronation.

SANDRO:

They say her coach is solid gold and drawn by eight grey horses.

THE DIPLOMAT:

May I ask you where you were going in such a hurry?

SANDRO:

I was going to see my father. He's rich enough to pay for the best suite on the entire ship but not rich enough to keep his promises. He promised me a real man's suit. A black serge suit with yellow pinstripes. I went through all my trunks and didn't find my suit.

THE DIPLOMAT:
You look familiar to me.

SANDRO:
Well, I've never seen you before, if I had I'd remember. And everyone knows I have an amazing memory.

THE DIPLOMAT:
Oh, really?

SANDRO:
The *Empress of France* weighs 20,123 tons, is 582 feet long by 75 feet wide by 42 feet high. The ship was built in Liverpool in 1928. Before the war, it was called the *Duchess of Bedford*. It was renamed the *Empress of France* after the war. This is its two-hundred-and-twenty-second voyage. (*Beat.*) I know lots of people who would have stopped listening to me and walked away by now. (*THE DIPLOMAT smiles at him.*) You need a good memory if you want to succeed in business. Never write anything down. Don't leave any traces. Remember everything. The captain has started to teach me the list of all the provisions on board.

THE DIPLOMAT:
Oh, really?

SANDRO:
24,430 pounds of flour, 7,350 pounds of cereal—

THE DIPLOMAT:
Certainly you don't intend to—

SANDRO:

When I've finished memorizing the whole list, it will be a great moment.

THE DIPLOMAT:

Do you always talk this much?

SANDRO:

Louise used to say that to me, too.

THE DIPLOMAT:

Who?

SANDRO:

(*putting on his glasses*) You see that steeple? She lives right near there. (*Proudly.*) She's seventeen. I'll be fourteen next month. As we speak, she's crying her heart out for me. I told her I'm leaving and she listened to me the way a woman listens to a man; *senza fare demande*—asking no questions.

THE DIPLOMAT:

Very impressive.

SANDRO:

Maybe you don't realize it, but I'm worth eleven thousand dollars.

THE DIPLOMAT:

Consider yourself lucky to know your worth. You have the answer to one of life's most important questions. Now I know where I've seen you. You're the Chief's son!

SANDRO:

You know my father?

THE DIPLOMAT:

In the beginning of time, when Archangel Michael banished Satan from heaven, before descending to the depths of the earth, Satan dug a hole to sow his seed. They say that your father's mother wallowed in the devil's seed, and so it came to pass that she gave birth to your father.

SANDRO:

Wow!

THE DIPLOMAT:

The Chief of Chiefs, the Captain of Vice, the King of Darkness. They say that God himself personally appointed the first cardinal of Montreal with the sole objective of banishing your father from the city.

SANDRO:

I'm the son of his Italian mistress. My brother is the son of his French mistress. Don't tell anybody, but we're fleeing the country.

THE DIPLOMAT:

I know. Here's your new passport, Sandro.

THE DIPLOMAT takes a passport out of his vest pocket.

SANDRO:

That's my picture! "Martin Peacock?" Are you the one we're paying eleven thousand dollars to find me such an ugly name?

THE DIPLOMAT:

I'm going to change my clothes.

SANDRO:

Go change your clothes.

THE DIPLOMAT:

We'll see each other again later today.

SANDRO:

We'll see each other again later today.

THE DIPLOMAT:

Please don't start that again.

SANDRO:

Please don't start—I'm just kidding.

THE DIPLOMAT:

Later on, we'll go to the ship's tailor.

SANDRO:

Your suit is a point of honour for me.

THE DIPLOMAT:

Well, I intend to give you that black serge suit with yellow pinstripes.

SANDRO:

Are you serious?

THE DIPLOMAT:

Yes!

SANDRO:

You promise?

THE DIPLOMAT:

I promise! Your father is right, those glasses are not flattering. They hide your eyes.

SANDRO:

For someone who almost got knocked over, you've been very nice.

Fog horn.

Episode 2

The Empress Room.

A table set for four. THE CHIEF is seated, back to the audience, smoking a cigar. WILLY is standing near the table. The table setting is exaggerated. THE BIOGRAPHER is standing near THE CHIEF.

THE BIOGRAPHER:
> Several weeks before the voyage, the Chief of Chiefs had offered to let me record his life for future generations. Bogged down for years in official speechwriting, lending my style to men who had no voice, I'd accepted his exciting offer to be the registrar of his past. (*Fog horn.*)

THE CHIEF:
> Did you hear the departure signal? We still haven't moved an inch. And the diplomat is late!

THE BIOGRAPHER:
> He'd confided all the stages of his rise in the hierarchy of the underworld.

THE CHIEF:
> When I invite people to eat with me, they usually arrive early.

THE BIOGRAPHER:
> I'd kept a detailed record of the names of all the martyrs sacrificed to the edification of his success.

THE CHIEF:

That's the second time we've heard the departure signal.

THE BIOGRAPHER:

His past was impressive. So successful, so young.

THE CHIEF:

"So successful, so young!" That's great stuff! (*Fog horn.*) You hear that?

THE BIOGRAPHER:

Montreal is holding you back. She can't forgive you for leaving.

THE CHIEF:

I like it.

THE BIOGRAPHER:

Two months earlier, this voyage, meant to be the most flamboyant of his entire career, had been transformed by a series of incidents into sombre exile.

THE CHIEF:

Sombre exile?

THE BIOGRAPHER:

When we boarded the ship, I suddenly grasped my daunting task: recording for posterity the decline and the fall of the Captain of Vice.

THE CHIEF:

Sombre exile! Decline! Fall! Find other words! Passage. Stage. Change. Make it sound better!

THE BIOGRAPHER:

I'm trying, sir.

THE CHIEF:
Use beautiful adjectives.

THE BIOGRAPHER:
I've already gone overboard on the superlatives!

THE CHIEF:
Just follow the example of our history books!

THE BIOGRAPHER:
What history books?

THE CHIEF:
Make my life story sound like one of our national heroes!

THE BIOGRAPHER:
What heroes?

THE CHIEF:
Don't ask me. Find one! Choose the juiciest details, the ones that feed envy. Make the entire Montreal Mafia jealous.

THE BIOGRAPHER:
Sir, there are two categories of biography: those that have been embellished and are sent for pulping, and those that tell the truth, the ones that survive.

THE CHIEF:
I don't want people to forget me. With my new passport, I'm going to disappear behind someone else's name. I want people to remember that I was great. Make everything bigger, better, grander!

THE BIOGRAPHER:
We have to maintain a minimum of objectivity.

THE CHIEF:

> Leave that to the police archives. And at the end, you'll write about my disappearance the way they write about life's great mysteries.

THE BIOGRAPHER:

> (*resigned*) On the other side of the ocean, a fascinating new life, full of surprises and unexpected events, awaited the illustrious mafioso.

THE CHIEF:

> It's beginning to sound better already!

THE BIOGRAPHER:

> At that very moment, his oldest son appeared. It was noon.

> *ÉTIENNE enters, wearing gloves.*

THE CHIEF:

> Just look at this, Étienne. The main lounge on the *Empress of France*, all to ourselves. This is where Princess Elizabeth drank her tea two years ago. And that's where the Duke of Edinburgh read his newspaper. This is going to be a crossing fit for kings. We're going to travel first class all the way. You'll see. Over there in England, we'll get a fresh start. This is the most important breakfast of our lives. Today marks the disappearance of our family. I want it to be a solemn occasion!

THE BIOGRAPHER:

> Grandiose!

THE CHIEF:

> The order for the narcotics had been placed by the vicar of Saint Madeleine's in Outremont. The vicar, in person! A clergyman caught with thirty-two

ounces of heroin. I promised the police an exceptional coup.

THE BIOGRAPHER:
You kept your promise!

THE CHIEF:
The churchbells of Montreal are still trembling... We were the most powerful. I remember King George's visit in 1939. He was supposed to stay on the second floor of the Hotel Windsor. Across the street from his room, there was a gambling parlour. So as not to spoil the monarch's view, they wanted to close the place down. They finally had to ask the king to change rooms instead.

ÉTIENNE:
History will remember you, Papa. (*Beat.*) Thanks to you, his biographer!

THE BIOGRAPHER :
History doesn't need me.

ÉTIENNE:
If history didn't need you, we wouldn't have to listen to him rehashing all this.

> *Beat.*

THE BIOGRAPHER:
(*withdrawing slightly*) The marching band on the quay struck up a new tune.

THE CHIEF:
The diplomat is late, but as soon as he arrives—

ÉTIENNE:
I'll go find your diplomat.

THE CHIEF:

A few minutes with me and you're already bored?

ÉTIENNE:

I'll bring him here right away.

THE CHIEF:

Stay here. I want you to learn how this business works.

ÉTIENNE:

What business? If you want to do business with a diplomat, you need a diplomat. I'm offering to find you a diplomat. Once the diplomat's here, I'll learn how the business works, and by the time I've learned as much as you, it will be my children's turn to get slaughtered! What do you say?

THE CHIEF:

You look pale.

ÉTIENNE:

Does that bother you?

THE CHIEF:

You're looking thin.

ÉTIENNE:

I've always been like this.

THE CHIEF:

You're acting arrogant.

ÉTIENNE:

That's recent.

THE CHIEF:

You leaving a girlfriend behind?

ÉTIENNE:

No.

THE CHIEF:

That's why you look pale.

ÉTIENNE:

Oh, really?

THE CHIEF:

You get the thinness from your mother. She was the thinnest one. Just wait, I'll find a woman for you, you'll see.

ÉTIENNE:

(*indicating his hands*) Since when are girls interested in cripples?

THE CHIEF:

Don't answer back like that!

ÉTIENNE:

"Sir, would you mind caressing my girlfriend for me. I can't do it myself."

THE CHIEF:

Don't answer back like that!

ÉTIENNE:

Or what? "Don't answer back like that" or what?

THE BIOGRAPHER:

A flock of gulls flew over the glass cupola of the main lounge.

THE CHIEF:

History is made up of wounds and disappointments.

ÉTIENNE:

Right!

THE BIOGRAPHER:

A warm breeze caressed the ship's decks.

THE CHIEF:
  History is made up of victories and losses.

ÉTIENNE:
  Right!

THE CHIEF:
  You should respect your father.

THE BIOGRAPHER:
  The son kissed his father.

ÉTIENNE:
  (*immobile*) Consider it done! I love you! Consider it said! Any other debts? (*Peering at* THE CHIEF's *face*) Some day they'll read the wrinkles on faces the way they read the lines of the hand. They'll say your wrinkles, the ones between your eyebrows, revealed a kind of apprehensive intelligence. The ones on your forehead will show that you lived in constant fear. The lines around your mouth will show that you often gritted your teeth with remorse. But they'll find no sign of the good father, no trace of the man who made his children laugh with his extravagant gestures, no trace of the man who protected them.

THE CHIEF:
  We'll build a better future for ourselves.

ÉTIENNE:
  Sounds like propaganda for conscription.

THE CHIEF:
  I thought you were taking medication!

ÉTIENNE:
  It masks the pain—

THE CHIEF:

Where's your medication?!

ÉTIENNE:

—not the outrage!

THE CHIEF:

You'll see, when we arrive in London—

ÉTIENNE:

(*shouting*) What will we do in London? What could we possibly do there that would be better than giving a concert? You go to London to play piano, to play for the Queen, to be applauded. Not to hide. London means notes and crescendos. Not a family in exile.

THE CHIEF:

Close all the doors!

ÉTIENNE:

I was a pianist! A great pianist!

THE CHIEF:

I don't want the diplomat to see him in this state.

ÉTIENNE:

They hailed me as Chopin's great disciple!

THE CHIEF:

I hate this kind of outburst!

ÉTIENNE:

I was supposed to play for the Queen! I was supposed to play at the Coronation Gala!

THE CHIEF:

Stop whining! We're going to the Coronation.

ÉTIENNE:

There were two of them. Two of them, behind me. Two faceless men. "Keep playing, we love music, keep playing!" One of them grabbed my wrists and held my hands down on the keyboard. "Keep playing, we told you to go on playing." The other one closed the cover ... on my hands. On my hands! Again and again! (*Shouting.*) Write that, Mr. Biographer! Again and again! Until the keyboard cover came off its hinges, until my finger bones burst out of my knuckles. The keyboard was red. My hands were red. I didn't know what was happening to me. I didn't understand. Those were my hands. There must be some mistake! Some mistake! And then ... then I saw the light. Why. And that was more painful than the injury itself. "We warned your father, told him to keep his big mouth shut. We told him to stop squealing on people." I was paying for my father. Paying for my father's incriminations. I would have preferred to be punished for my talent. Write that, Mr. Biographer! The royal suite, the Empress Room, exile in luxury—all courtesy of the Montreal police for services rendered!

THE CHIEF:

We've always lived in luxury.

ÉTIENNE:

With my music, I'd managed to forget the brawls in back alleys, the noisy drinking bouts, the pleading of whores being taught a lesson.

THE CHIEF:

Regrets prevent you from acting, prevent you from thinking straight.

ÉTIENNE:

Through my music, I'd managed to forget that your world would catch up with me sooner or later.

THE CHIEF:

Étienne, I never thought they'd carry out their threats.

ÉTIENNE:

(*devastated*) You knew?!

THE CHIEF:

I know everything.

ÉTIENNE:

You knew I was in danger.

THE BIOGRAPHER:

The day before we set sail, the police had padlocked the last brothels, burned the last gambling tables. Montreal the Whore was once again becoming Montreal the Saint.

THE CHIEF:

I'll make you both happy over there.

ÉTIENNE:

You knew!

THE CHIEF:

I'll give you both the best of everything. There's nothing left for us here. Small-time pimps, beggars, churchmice, honky-tonk hicks, hewers of wood, stray dogs. Hundreds of words in their mouths, a nickel in one pocket, their rosary beads in the other. Business will be better over there. It's too small here. No style. I'm going to give you the best of everything. Better names, better lives. We'll get a fresh start, over there.

ÉTIENNE:

Some day they'll discover the truth by reading the lines on your face, not your biography.

THE CHIEF:

You'll forget. You'll see, sooner or later, we forget everything.

ÉTIENNE:

I've got a title for your memoirs. "A Lesson in Impotence."

THE CHIEF:

You know I love you!

ÉTIENNE:

Right! That will make a great chapter.

Long silence.

THE BIOGRAPHER:

Should I embellish all that, sir?

THE CHIEF:

Stay here, Étienne!

THE BIOGRAPHER:

Not one of his mistresses came to see him off.

THE CHIEF:

You can drop that last sentence.

THE BIOGRAPHER:

The diplomat entered the Empress Room a few minutes early.

THE DIPLOMAT enters. He has changed his clothes.

THE DIPLOMAT:

Sorry to be late!

THE CHIEF:
  My saviour! Whisky?

THE DIPLOMAT:
  (greeting ÉTIENNE) I've had the pleasure of hearing
  you play, sir. Bravi! Bravi! (to THE CHIEF) We're
  going to witness world history.

THE CHIEF:
  If this ship ever sets sail!

THE DIPLOMAT:
  Such a young queen!

THE CHIEF:
  The hope of the entire Empire. (*Beat.*) Did
  everything go smoothly?

  *THE DIPLOMAT gives WILLY a tip, indicating that he
  can leave. WILLY exits.*

THE DIPLOMAT:
  I have the passports in safekeeping.

THE CHIEF:
  What do you mean, "in safekeeping?"

THE DIPLOMAT:
  They say that anyone who dines with you is court-
  ing the devil.

THE BIOGRAPHER:
  There's our prologue, sir!

THE CHIEF:
  Where are our passports?

  THE DIPLOMAT sits down.

THE BIOGRAPHER:
  The diplomat made himself comfortable.

THE DIPLOMAT:

They say the Canadian delegation to the Coronation is more imposing that those sent to the consecration of our cardinal in Rome and the funerals of Stalin, Queen Mary and Evita Peron all put together.

THE CHIEF:

(*straight to the point*) Okay! What do you want? A bonus? How much?

THE DIPLOMAT:

I enjoy doing business with people like you, Mr. Peacock.

THE CHIEF:

Peacock?

THE BIOGRAPHER:

The proudest, most regal of all birds, sir.

ÉTIENNE:

The vainest, too.

THE DIPLOMAT:

You were born in Gloucester. You're a widower. Your sons' names are James and Martin.

THE CHIEF:

Did you hear that, Étienne? Your name is James. (*to The Diplomat*) How much is your bonus?

THE DIPLOMAT:

Should we settle this in front of your son?

THE CHIEF:

A son should see how his father does business.

THE DIPLOMAT:

As you wish.

THE CHIEF:

   The police already paid you eleven thousand dollars per passport. How much is your bonus?

THE DIPLOMAT:

   I want you to put me in touch with someone.

THE CHIEF:

   Who? I'm leaving the country.

THE DIPLOMAT:

   I recently met a charming individual. I was overwhelmed by a deep emotion. A painful emotion. I had to lower my head, for fear someone would notice me blushing.

THE CHIEF:

   Who?

THE DIPLOMAT:

   I need your permission to prolong the seduction. You'll get your passports afterwards.

THE CHIEF:

   Who is it?

THE DIPLOMAT:

   Your family's freedom in exchange for one night with your youngest son, Sandro. I usually meet my under-age lovers in dark, dirty places, in windowless cubbyholes. Cheerless faces. Sandro is clean and he smells good.

THE BIOGRAPHER:

   The King of Vice suddenly felt faint. He braced himself on an armchair.

THE CHIEF:

   Is this some kind of joke?

THE DIPLOMAT:
No.

THE CHIEF:
You're sick.

THE DIPLOMAT:
Dethroned kings can't afford to bite the hand that saves them.

THE CHIEF:
Étienne, don't you have business to attend to?

ÉTIENNE:
I was asked to stay here.

THE DIPLOMAT:
I'd like to tell you I'm doing this to avenge my sister the whore who was beaten to a pulp by your thugs, or my brother who died of a heroin overdose, or my other brother driven to his grave by gambling debts and gunshots, but I'm an only child. No. I have no reason other than the beautiful eyes of your youngest son.

THE BIOGRAPHER:
With a feeble gesture, the Captain of Vice begged the diplomat to be quiet.

THE DIPLOMAT:
Don't look at me that way. I won't lower my eyes. Over the years, I've learned to bury any remorse. You must know what I mean. I have to admit that this is an incredible moment for me—you are about to give me permission to seduce your son. I don't have to worry about his denouncing me, since I'm asking you to be my accomplice. It's strange but marvellous.

THE BIOGRAPHER:
The King of Darkness wanted to pounce on the diplomat.

THE DIPLOMAT:
Careful! They say emotions are forbidden in your profession. I'm afraid the titillation might lose its edge. You know what I mean—there's something titillating about committing an act that is illegal and immoral. It's always a delightful sensation.

THE CHIEF hasn't budged.

THE BIOGRAPHER:
He couldn't remain silent.

THE DIPLOMAT:
Have you forgotten what the pianist just endured? They say he'll never play again.

ÉTIENNE:
(*coldly*) He'll never play again.

THE BIOGRAPHER:
(*commenting*) Silence.

THE DIPLOMAT:
You talked too much.

THE BIOGRAPHER:
Silence.

THE DIPLOMAT:
They'll hunt you down to the ends of the earth. You didn't play by the rules, Chief.

THE BIOGRAPHER:
Silence.

THE DIPLOMAT:
You talk too much.

THE BIOGRAPHER:
Silence.

THE DIPLOMAT:
These passports are the best money can buy. Think about your future, or at least your children's future.

THE BIOGRAPHER:
More silence.

THE DIPLOMAT:
Good fortune and prosperity await you over there.

THE BIOGRAPHER:
The Chief of Chiefs banged both fists down on the table!

THE DIPLOMAT:
I want him to feel comfortable with me. Can you tell me more about his girlfriend Louise? It would help me create an atmosphere of intimacy. (*Silence.*) You'll see, it's not so tragic. He'll recover. Afterwards, they always feel as if they played at something they couldn't quite grasp. Their smiles are different, so are their eyes. Some of them become withdrawn, others grow to like it. But they all grow up a bit faster. It's a pity they can't keep that inner fragility a bit longer. Of course, if everything goes smoothly, I'll hide your collaboration from him. Do you know that he has an amazing memory? I don't expect you to give me an answer today. But don't wait too long. England is closer than you think. (*Fog horn.*) It's not too late to leave the boat.

THE BIOGRAPHER:
He offered him all the money in the world.

THE DIPLOMAT:

> I know from experience that your historian will transform this incident. Historians always disagree on one point: history.

THE BIOGRAPHER:

> He grabbed him by the neck. He tore out his eyes. He stabbed him to death.

THE DIPLOMAT:

> I can understand your pain. I've known pain myself. I can understand your feeling horrified. But you'll be amazed. We can get used to anything. Tell yourself that in sacrificing your youngest son, it's just another son being sacrificed.

THE CHIEF:

> Stop smiling, Étienne.

ÉTIENNE:

> I thought this trip was going be a dreadful bore. But suddenly I'm eager to see how your inimitable talents will get us out of this mess. We can't leave the ship now, they'll shoot us down on the quay. Without our passports, we can't leave the ship in Liverpool either. You can't shoot the diplomat, we don't know where the passports are. And neither you, and certainly not I, can torture him. What an incredible voyage it's going to be. (*gravely*) I simply hope for your sake that Sandro will find a way to forget.

THE BIOGRAPHER:

> Not a word, not a gesture.

> *SANDRO enters, wearing his glasses.*

SANDRO:

(*to his father*) I checked twice. I searched all three trunks, the brown one and both green ones. I didn't find a black suit with yellow pinstripes. And I was wearing my glasses.

THE CHIEF:

This is no time to piss me off.

SANDRO:

Mentanare la promessa? Canadese!

THE CHIEF:

I don't understand Italian, Sandro.

SANDRO:

A black suit with yellow pinstripes!

THE CHIEF:

I had more important things to think about than your wardrobe!

SANDRO:

(*angrily*) *Basta!* Lots of boys my age would be happy to have a father like mine, a father who can buy them anything they want. But nobody would want a father who doesn't keep his promises. (*glancing at THE DIPLOMAT*) I met someone who will give me my suit.

THE CHIEF:

Who?

SANDRO:

Someone! (*to THE DIPLOMAT*) Hello, sir. Is everything working out as you hoped?

THE DIPLOMAT:

Everything is working out.

SANDRO:

Have you given him our passports?

THE DIPLOMAT:

Not yet.

SANDRO:

(*to his father*) That's right, I know everything! You have to give me some money, I need to have a suit cleaned. What's the matter, Étienne?

ÉTIENNE:

Nothing. Nothing's the matter. My hands hurt. That's all.

THE BIOGRAPHER:

Long silence.

THE DIPLOMAT:

I'll leave you with your family. I don't want to miss the ship's departure. (*He exits.*)

THE CHIEF:

We'll find a solution.

ÉTIENNE:

A solution?

SANDRO:

Are you talking about my black suit?

THE CHIEF:

(*to SANDRO*) That's right. We're talking about your suit. (*moved*) Such a nice face, it reminds me of your mother. But you spoil it with your glasses.

SANDRO:

This is no time to remind me of a woman I left behind yesterday in order to follow you.

ÉTIENNE:

Sandro, you know how much our father loves us!

SANDRO:

La mamma ha detto: attento a tuo padre, lui si ricorda
di avere un cuore ogni volta che i suoi affari vanno male.

THE CHIEF:

Don't speak Italian to me!

SANDRO:

Mamma says: Watch out for your father, the only
time he ever remembers he has a heart is when he's
in trouble.

Étienne exits.

THE BIOGRAPHER:

(*looking at* THE CHIEF) Silence!

Fog horn.

First-class deck. The military band is playing in the background. THE MINISTER, his wife ALICE and their daughter MARGUERITE approach the railing. They will be joined by MADEMOISELLE LAVALLÉE, protocol officer on the Empress of France.

THE MINISTER:
Smile, Marguerite.

MARGUERITE:
I'm smiling.

ALICE:
Smile harder, Marguerite. Your public life has started.

MADEMOISELLE LAVALLÉE:
(*as she hands them Union Jack flags*) The Honourable Minister Gendron! Madame Gendron! Wave your flags and look toward Pier 14! That's where the photographers are.

THE MINISTER:
We have to make sure people see we're on board.

ALICE:
And happy to be here, I suppose?

MADEMOISELLE LAVALLÉE:
The Queen has asked the Royal Air Force to change the course of the planes that are supposed to fly over Buckingham Palace after the Coronation.

THE MINISTER:
Really!

MADEMOISELLE LAVALLÉE:
She doesn't want her crown to fall off when she lifts her head to watch them.

THE MINISTER:
Fantastic! Did you hear that, Alice?

ALICE:
Mademoiselle Lavallée?

MADEMOISELLE LAVALLÉE:
Madame Gendron?

ALICE:
Who assigned our seats at Westminster Abbey?

MADEMOISELLE LAVALLÉE:
We did, Madame Gendron.

ALICE:
Facing a wall? We were told that the Canadian delegation will spend nine hours facing a wall unable to see any of the Coronation ceremony. What are we supposed to say when we get back? That the Queen was Gothic, dark and stony, and that it's high time the place was cleaned?

MADEMOISELLE LAVALLÉE:
I'll see what I can do.

ALICE:
Don't see, do! We gave three sons to England, that must be worth three good seats for the show!

MADEMOISELLE LAVALLÉE:
Of course, Madame Gendron. (*to* THE MINISTER) Here's the list of your duties in London.

THE MINISTER:

(*reading*) Weekend at Viscount and Lady Alexander's country estate.

MADEMOISELLE LAVALLÉE:

(*reading*) Dinner with Prime Ministers Saint-Laurent and Churchill, and the other distinguished federal ministers, at the National Gallery.

THE MINISTER:

Tea in the Royal tent at Buckingham Palace—

ALICE:

Mademoiselle Lavallée, I'd also like you to explain our inexplicable absence at the Captain's table.

MADEMOISELLE LAVALLÉE:

I'll see what I can do. (*turning back to* THE MINISTER) A guided tour—

ALICE:

I haven't finished!

THE MINISTER:

(*annoyed*) She hasn't finished.

ALICE:

At the dinner at Canada House in London, according to the seating plan, you assigned us seats next to the enormous Queen Salote of Tonga. Don't you realize that she snores during meals?

MADEMOISELLE LAVALLÉE:

I'll see what I can do!

ALICE:

Don't see, do!

MADEMOISELLE LAVALLÉE:

Anything else?

ALICE:
Yes.

MARGUERITE:
Mama, please!

ALICE:
The boat!

MADEMOISELLE LAVALLÉE:
What about the boat?

ALICE:
Is it going to rust at the dock?

MADEMOISELLE LAVALLÉE:
The Indians!

ALICE:
What about the Indians?

MADEMOISELLE LAVALLÉE:
Nobody's seen the Indians board. And we can't sail
without them!

ALICE:
There are other boats!

MADEMOISELLE LAVALLÉE:
Can you see us arriving in London with no Indians?
A Canadian boat with no Indians?

ALICE:
Well, go find them!

MARGUERITE:
Mama!

MADEMOISELLE LAVALLÉE:
I'll see what I can do, ma'am.

ALICE:

Where did you learn the ground rules of protocol, Mademoiselle Lavallée? In the *Reader's Digest* Book of the Month?

MADEMOISELLE LAVALLÉE:

No, at Rideau Hall. And do you know what the most important thing I learned was?

ALICE:

No.

MADEMOISELLE LAVALLÉE:

I used to say: "Get off my back!" Now I say: "I'll see what I can do." (*as she exits*) Flags! Flags! Who wants a flag!

THE MINISTER:

Alice, are you going to carry on like this for the whole trip?

ALICE:

I've decided to take charge of your political career. And if you run in the next election—

THE MINISTER:

I am running in the next election.

ALICE:

I'm going to take charge of your campaign!

> *THE DIPLOMAT appears on the deck, carrying his cage with the birds. He greets THE MINISTER, his wife and daughter.*

THE DIPLOMAT:

Mr. Minister, Madame Gendron.

THE MINISTER:

Good morning, sir.

THE DIPLOMAT:
Mademoiselle Gendron.

THE MINISTER:
(*noticing his daughter's distraction*) Marguerite!

MARGUERITE:
Good morning, sir!

THE MINISTER:
My daughter will be representing our country at the Coronation gala.

THE DIPLOMAT:
Congratulations.

MARGUERITE:
In fact, I'm replacing another pianist.

THE MINISTER:
Say thank you, Marguerite.

MARGUERITE:
Thank you.

THE MINISTER:
We're very proud of her.

ALICE:
So many years of effort, the lessons, the Conservatory, all the sacrifices, so she can play for the Queen of England. Had we known, we would've chosen the bagpipes. (*to THE DIPLOMAT*) What a horrible idea, keeping birds in a cage!

THE DIPLOMAT:
They were born in captivity.

ALICE:
Weren't we all, sir.

THE MINISTER:
Is your wife travelling with you?

THE DIPLOMAT:
No. The flu.

THE MINISTER:
Did you hear that, Alice? Our friend's wife has the flu.

ALICE:
Do wish your wife a speedy recovery.

THE MINISTER:
Marguerite!

MARGUERITE:
Do wish your wife a speedy recovery.

Long silence.

THE MINISTER:
Does she get the flu often?

ALICE:
Joseph! We've done our bit.

THE MINISTER:
Tell me, have we ever been introduced?

ALICE:
Don't tell me you're going to introduce yourself to all the passengers? Seven days on board, a thousand passengers. Wait till the Prime Minister calls the elections before you start playing the clown. (*to* THE DIPLOMAT) We're always being introduced to someone. We spend our lives shaking hands and washing our own afterwards. That's what they call politics in Canada. After all these years, I'm still trying to figure out what makes a politician

so charismatic—why does a voter feel transformed by a single handshake from someone who's been elected?

THE DIPLOMAT:
The Captain forecasts a smooth sailing.

THE MINISTER:
That's because he doesn't know my wife.

ALICE:
The last time I crossed the Atlantic, it was to take flowers to my sons' graves in France.

THE MINISTER:
We lost our sons in Dieppe.

THE DIPLOMAT:
The 1942 massacre or the victory in '44?

THE MINISTER:
'42.

ALICE:
The massacre.

THE DIPLOMAT:
The flower of youth.

THE MINISTER:
The flower of youth.

ALICE:
For the greater good of England!

THE MINISTER:
For the greater good of Europe!

ALICE:
A Canadian drama.

THE MINISTER:
> We had to help Churchill!

ALICE:
> A British drama.

THE MINISTER:
> We had to help Stalin!

ALICE:
> A Russian drama! My own husband's government authorized the Dieppe landing. Pierre, twenty-two years old, Paul, eighteen, and Arthur.

THE MINISTER:
> Arthur is still alive!

ALICE:
> A lump of a man. There's no room left on his body to pin the medals. All we have left is one daughter and she's going to play for the Queen of England.

MARGUERITE:
> Time for me to put some things away in my cabin.

THE MINISTER:
> Marguerite.

MARGUERITE:
> I'm afraid you'll have to excuse me, but I have some things to put away in my cabin.

THE MINISTER:
> Stay with us. I want you to see how your father honours his responsibilities.

THE DIPLOMAT:
> They say it's going to be raining in London.

ALICE:
The sun was shining in Dieppe. The Germans had a fabulous view of the beach.

THE MINISTER:
There'll be nine young Canadian women in the Coronation choir at Westminster Abbey.

THE DIPLOMAT:
I didn't know that.

ALICE:
It was the Queen's cousin, her husband's favourite uncle, Lord Mountbatten, who improvised the Dieppe landing.

THE MINISTER:
(*brief pause*) CBC is going to be the first network in North America to broadcast the entire coronation ceremony. With only a twelve-hour delay thanks to an impressive relay of planes.

THE DIPLOMAT:
I hope they don't play music over the Coronation coverage.

THE MINISTER:
Don't you like music?

THE DIPLOMAT:
During the war, there was always music on the newsreels that arrived from Europe.

THE MINISTER:
Yes, proud music.

THE DIPLOMAT:
Proud, reassuring, sometimes even triumphant music and the commentary on our losses was almost enthusiastic. You couldn't hear the prayers,

the fearful panting, the lungs gasping their last breath, nor the parting words, the words we had to take back to the mothers, the widows and orphans, nor the cries of youth perishing. Nothing. None of that ever crossed the Atlantic. Back here, music buried the sound of History. Over there, the soldiers were cannon fodder. Back here, they were a melody. Meanwhile the politicians handled everything else in silence. I hope they don't play music over the Coronation coverage. It would be dangerous if people found the whole thing reassuring. Nine young Canadian women burying the voices of thousands of corpses.

THE MINISTER:
I don't understand.

THE DIPLOMAT:
I was in Dieppe during the massacre. I probably met your sons' souls there. Madam, Mr. Minister.

He moves away.

THE MINISTER:
What a strange man!

ALICE:
I rather like him. What did you say his name was?

THE MINISTER:
I don't know. We didn't have time to introduce ourselves. (*ÉTIENNE enters and comes to lean on the rail.*) Are you coming, Alice!

ALICE:
I like it here.

THE MINISTER:
The photographers have changed place. Come.

MARGUERITE:

(*She only has eyes for ÉTIENNE.*) I'll be right there.

THE MINISTER and his wife move away. MARGUERITE joins ÉTIENNE at the rail.

MARGUERITE:

I've never taken a boat before. I'm afraid I'm going to be seasick, but they say the sea is calmer in the spring. The people on the quays envy us.

ÉTIENNE:

Small-time pimps, beggars, churchmice, honky-tonk hicks, hewers of wood, stray dogs...

MARGUERITE:

You shouldn't say that.

ÉTIENNE:

I said it.

MARGUERITE:

I'm Marguerite Gendron.

ÉTIENNE:

I don't want to know you.

MARGUERITE:

Say something nice to me.

ÉTIENNE:

Why should I say something nice to you?

MARGUERITE:

Try.

ÉTIENNE:

Your dress is clean.

MARGUERITE:

You're funny.

ÉTIENNE:

I'm not funny.

MARGUERITE:

I'm Marguerite Gendron.

ÉTIENNE:

I don't want to know you.

MARGUERITE:

I'm the one who's replacing you at the Coronation
gala.

ÉTIENNE:

(*hurt*) Would you mind tying my shoe lace for me?
It's because of my hands. I can't do it myself.

MARGUERITE:

Your laces are tied.

ÉTIENNE:

I could see in your eyes.

MARGUERITE:

What did you see?

ÉTIENNE:

You missed the pottery sale at the rehabilitation
centre. One lady bought two abstract sculptures.
But the poor lady didn't realize the artist had tried
to make salad bowls. It's because of his hands. He
can't do it. I could see in your eyes.

MARGUERITE:

What did you see in my eyes?

ÉTIENNE:

When you've had your share of admiring looks and
you have to get used to this other look, it's simple, I
can't do it.

MARGUERITE:

I should have begun by saying I'm terribly sorry about your hands.

ÉTIENNE:

Consider it said.

MARGUERITE:

I should have told you you were a great pianist.

ÉTIENNE:

Consider it done. Now leave me alone.

MARGUERITE:

The first time I heard you play was at the Music Circle at the Ritz Carlton. A wonderful recital. (*Looking at his hands.*) Arthritis?

ÉTIENNE:

No, it was Chopin.

MARGUERITE:

People warned me you were bitter.

ÉTIENNE:

So why don't you leave? Do you find bitterness attractive?

MARGUERITE:

I've always been so impressed by you!

ÉTIENNE:

Do you want to apologize for taking my place? For having jumped with joy when you heard about my misfortune?

MARGUERITE:

Don't think—

ÉTIENNE:

People are always waiting for someone to break his neck so they can take his place.

MARGUERITE:

I wouldn't want to—

ÉTIENNE:

Steal crumbs from the once great? Chalking up a few minutes of intimacy? I saw Chopin's Great Disciple! I saw his misery! I saw the failure!

MARGUERITE:

A while ago, when I saw you arrive on the deck—

ÉTIENNE:

I used to practice piano night and day, telling myself that failure would be the only way I'd ever get any rest, appease the chaos inside me, bring some respite to the passion and propel myself into real life ... But I've never been so nervous. I wake up exhausted. My dreams are litanies of complaints. Look at me. There is nothing but grief and sorrow.

MARGUERITE:

I didn't want to—

ÉTIENNE:

So what did you want, Marie?

MARGUERITE:

Marguerite!

ÉTIENNE:

I have no gift for remembering the names of second choices.

MARGUERITE:

I want Chopin! They gave me your place, but they also gave me your programme. Liszt is my love. I need you to teach me Chopin's secrets.

ÉTIENNE:

Chopin died for the second time two months ago.

MARGUERITE:

This gala is my big chance, the one that comes once in a lifetime.

ÉTIENNE:

How tactful!

MARGUERITE:

When they told me I'd be playing your programme, everything became dark.

ÉTIENNE:

Wear black.

MARGUERITE:

Chopin drapes himself in melancholy. He wears his broken heart on his sleeve. He corsets his soul till he swoons in exaltation. They can dress me in black, white or red, in so little time, I'll never be able to feel Chopin's colours inside me.

ÉTIENNE:

What do you need to play Chopin? An unhappy love affair? The hall will be full of aristocratic matrons whose diamonds are as loose as their dentures, false music lovers who mistake wrong notes for Bartok, phonies who attend concerts to show off their clothes. From the Queen down to you, there'll be nothing but pretense. Just make them think you've suffered. And don't forget.

During the applause, bow your head to the right, that's where the Queen will be. Then pick up the folds of your skirt and curtsy! If there's a tear in your eye, let it flow! Audiences love emotion. If the Queen claps her hands more than twenty times, your career is guaranteed throughout the Commonwealth, otherwise you'll be known as the "Canadian girl."

MARGUERITE:

Be my soul, I'll be your hands? (*Beat.*) In exchange, you can ask me for anything you want.

ÉTIENNE:

Make me happy.

MARGUERITE:

What?

ÉTIENNE:

Make me happy. Take the cynicism out of my smiles. Erase the sadness in my eyes. Make me believe that people are kind, that mothers worry about their children, that fathers watch over them ...

MARGUERITE:

I don't understand.

ÉTIENNE:

Do the impossible. Make this voyage pleasant for me. I'm not asking you to be the love that knows no bounds, the one that fulfills all fantasies. Be a passing fling, the love that soothes, that heals wounds. Be the love between two heartbeats, the love one uses for a while and then discards. I haven't known a woman's tenderness for so long. And it would make my father so happy.

MARGUERITE:
The hardness of your heart terrifies me.

ÉTIENNE:
Tell me your life story. Perhaps I'll find inspiration
to go on with mine. Choose the most touching
memories. Make it up, if you must.

MARGUERITE:
Make it up? That's insincere. Love is sincere. You
can't play with feelings.

ÉTIENNE:
My father tells me it comes with age.

MARGUERITE:
That's absurd.

ÉTIENNE:
Absurd? I have every reason in the world to leave
this boat and I'm still on board. That's absurd! Go
ahead, say something nice to me.

> *Several blasts of the foghorn. All the passengers arrive
> on the deck.*

MADEMOISELLE LAVALLÉE:
(*still distributing flags*) Wave your flags! The Indians
have finally boarded. We're about to sail. Look at
the photographers in front of Pier 18, wave your
flags and smile! (*to MARGUERITE*) Did you hear that
Princess Margaret will be representing the Queen
at the wedding of Princess Ragnhild of Norway
today. She is marrying Erling Lorentzen, a shipping
magnate!

MARGUERITE:
(*confused*) Fantastic!

MADEMOISELLE LAVALLÉE:

The cable says that Lorentzen said "I do" in a confident voice, and the princess replied in a faltering voice. I didn't realize that Princess Ragnhild was the only daughter of Crown Prince Olav of Norway. Did you?

MARGUERITE:

I didn't realize there was a monarchy in Norway!

MADEMOISELLE LAVALLÉE:

What do they teach you in the conservatories?!

ÉTIENNE:

They teach them how to imitate geniuses.

ÉLISABETH TURCOTTE:

The boat's moving!

ÉLISABETH MÉNARD:

The boat's moving! We're leaving.

ÉLISABETH TURCOTTE:

Quick, Élisabeth! We're leaving the port.

ÉLISABETH PENNINGTON:

(*as she enters*) I'm coming, I'm coming.

SANDRO:

(*to ÉTIENNE*) People are betting on the sailboat race on the starboard side. Can you give me some money?

ÉTIENNE:

No.

SANDRO:

You know, I wanted to visit you in the hospital, but my mother wouldn't let me. She said it was dangerous. But I thought about you a lot.

ÉTIENNE:

(*touched*) Really?

SANDRO:

I even thought of a new job for you—boxer. You might not be in shape for it, but you've got the right temperament. (*ÉTIENNE smiles.*)

ÉLISABETH TURCOTTE:

Gee, it's so high.

ÉLISABETH MÉNARD:

I can even see my street from here.

SANDRO:

I missed you. I really wanted to visit you in the hospital, but my mother wouldn't let me.

ÉTIENNE:

Sandro?

SANDRO:

Cosa?

ÉTIENNE:

Are you saying this to me for money?

SANDRO:

Just enough to make a bet.

ÉTIENNE:

You're disgusting. (*He gives him some money.*)

SANDRO:

Grazie!

The band plays "God Save the Queen."

MADEMOISELLE LAVALLÉE:

We're off! We're off!

THE MINISTER:
We're off, Alice!

THE CHIEF appears on the deck with his biographer.

ALICE:
Why, Joseph, there's one of your party's patrons!

THE MINISTER:
What is he doing on this ship?

ALICE:
Aren't you going to say hello?

THE MINISTER:
Haven't you read the newspapers?

ALICE:
Good day to you, Chief!

THE MINISTER:
(*distressed*) Alice! The photographers!

ÉTIENNE:
(*to his father*) Have you found a solution?

THE CHIEF:
It's all arranged.

ÉTIENNE:
What's the "solution?"

THE DIPLOMAT:
Sandro, come stand with me.

SANDRO:
Here I come. (*Showing him the money ÉTIENNE gave him.*) I have the money to get your suit cleaned.

ÉTIENNE:
(*sarcastically*) As you say, it seems to be "all arranged."

SANDRO:

(*to* MADEMOISELLE LAVALLÉE) Is that the national
anthem?

MADEMOISELLE LAVALLÉE:

It's "God Save the Queen!"

THE DIPLOMAT:

This music is frightening my birds.

ALICE:

It frightens the East Indians, the Pakistanis and the
French Canadians, too. (ALICE *goes to stand beside*
THE CHIEF.)

THE MINISTER:

Would you please stay here beside me.

ALICE:

We have a lovely view of the courthouse from here!

THE MINISTER:

Alice!!!

SANDRO:

Anchors aweigh!

THE BIOGRAPHER:

It was a huge white ship sailing forth between two
tides. The last world war had abolished what little
innocence mankind had retained.

THE DIPLOMAT:

The ship is leaving the port, Chief.

The three ÉLISABETHS *wave to people on the quay.*

ÉLISABETH TURCOTTE:

Élisabeth, look, that's my fiancé on the dock!

ÉLISABETH MÉNARD:

Mine's there, too, Élisabeth.

ÉLISABETH PENNINGTON:
(*less enthusiastically*) And there's my parents ...

THE MINISTER:
Marguerite, come stand with us.

MADEMOISELLE LAVALLÉE:
We're off! We're off!

THE DIPLOMAT:
Wave your flag, Sandro.

THE BIOGRAPHER:
From now on, every man and every woman would be a pawn on someone's chessboard. Everyone was prepared to bargain and everyone had his price. Nothing but old-fashioned symbols, like the promising future of a young queen being crowned, could renew our faith in a brighter tomorrow.

MARGUERITE:
Would you ... would you like me to hold your flag?

ÉTIENNE:
Such tact!

THE CHIEF:
(*to THE BIOGRAPHER*) Make it bigger, better, grander!

THE BIOGRAPHER:
They would soon leave their worries behind, free at last to admire the immensity and the power of the ocean. They would adapt their daily routine to match the ship's roll. Regular activities would punctuate every day: cinema, sporting competitions on the upper decks, cocktails, board games, formal balls, and most of all, lavish, beautifully prepared meals. Is that better, sir?

THE DIPLOMAT:
   Your flag, Sandro!

Episode 4

Smoking lounge.

One of the main doors to the ballroom is ajar,
illuminating the silhouette of THE CHIEF who is
smoking a cigar. He is listening to the music coming
from the ballroom. THE BIOGRAPHER is nearby.
Someone is rehearsing Chopin. There is a deep
sadness in the air.

THE BIOGRAPHER:

> The passengers had quickly unpacked their trunks,
> eager to check, once again, their outfits for the
> London festivities. The ship forged ahead calmly,
> with no apparent crises, no untimely incidents. The
> Chief of Chiefs had punctuated the passage down
> the St. Lawrence with memories of his exploits in
> each port. Shawinigan, a clever transaction.
> Rivière-du-Loup, a settling of accounts. Québec
> City, the dance halls and the conquest of so many
> lovely legs.

THE CHIEF:

> You can still manage to make up a good story?

THE BIOGRAPHER:

> It is the historian's task to interpret the hero's
> silences.

THE CHIEF:

> Look at me. How do you interpret tonight's
> silence?

THE BIOGRAPHER:

I have children, myself, sir, and …

THE CHIEF:

And?

THE BIOGRAPHER:

I try to be as close to them as possible. We try to tell each other the truth, and we look for solutions together.

THE CHIEF:

Sometimes I envy you ordinary people.

THE BIOGRAPHER:

Sandro entered with the horned larks. Before speaking to his father, he was careful to take off his glasses.

SANDRO enters. He takes off his glasses and slips them into his pocket.

THE CHIEF:

I don't want to see him.

SANDRO:

I'm already here, Papa.

THE BIOGRAPHER:

The Gulf of the St. Lawrence. Day 2 of the crossing. Evening. (*to THE CHIEF*) Shall I order you a whisky, sir?

He exits.

SANDRO:

I waited for you in the dining room.

THE CHIEF:

You waited for me?

SANDRO:
Weren't you hungry?

THE CHIEF:
I wasn't hungry.

SANDRO:
You missed the minister's wife making a scene.

THE CHIEF:
She made a scene?

SANDRO:
She wanted to be seated at the Captain's table.
(*Beat.*) The Captain gave her his place.

THE CHIEF:
I missed all that.

SANDRO:
Is that the substitute who's playing?

THE CHIEF:
Who?

SANDRO:
That's what Étienne calls her.

THE CHIEF:
I don't know who's playing.

SANDRO:
The fog has lifted. We've left the lights on the
North Shore behind.

THE CHIEF:
Already?

SANDRO:
It's very dark.

THE CHIEF:
 Really?

SANDRO:
 Étienne is still on the deck.

THE CHIEF:
 Still in the same place?

SANDRO:
 He spent the whole night there.

THE CHIEF:
 It's because of his hands.

SANDRO:
 You should tell him to come inside. (*speaking of the birds*) They're horned larks. The big one is called Pacific. The other one is Atlantic.

THE CHIEF:
 People take dogs for walks, not birds.

SANDRO:
 He's known a lot of women.

THE CHIEF:
 Who has?

SANDRO:
 The diplomat. He showed me some pictures. They're very good-looking. But the prettiest one is his wife.

THE CHIEF:
 There are lots of young people your age on the boat, you could have a good time with them, instead of hanging out in some diplomat's cabin.

SANDRO:
 259 first-class cabins, 441 tourist-class.

THE CHIEF:
  Sandro!

SANDRO:
  Quattro saloni, tre sale da pranzo, due sale da ballo—

THE CHIEF:
  Stop!

SANDRO:
  It's the first time someone important has been
  interested in me.

THE CHIEF:
  Put your glasses back on!

SANDRO:
  You say I look ugly with my glasses.

THE CHIEF:
  You can see him again, if you wear your glasses.

SANDRO:
  I'm allowed to see him? *Grazie!* (*quickly correcting
  himself*) Thanks!

THE CHIEF:
  Have you and I ever had a real talk?

SANDRO:
  Isn't that what we're doing now?

THE CHIEF:
  A man to man talk.

SANDRO:
  Sure, we talk about all sorts of unimportant things,
  but that's how men talk to each other, isn't it?

THE CHIEF:
  You know, sometimes in life, you have to make big
  sacrifices for other people.

SANDRO:

And I'm making a big one for you.

Beat.

THE CHIEF:

(*worried*) What do you mean?

SANDRO:

I know everything. The diplomat explained everything to me.

THE CHIEF:

What do you know?

SANDRO:

I know that forgetting Louise is a big sacrifice I'm
making so I can follow you. (*Beat.*) Are you crying?

THE CHIEF:

It's the music.

SANDRO:

One day, God appeared to a man whose faith was
unshakeable. He said. "Sharpen your knife, prepare
the wood for a burnt offering, lay it on your son's
back and lead him to the highest mountain. When
you have reached the summit, immolate your son,
your beloved son, as a sacrifice to me." The man
sharpened his knife, chopped the wood and led his
son to the mountain. That is when the son asked
the father what animal he was going to sacrifice.
Which sheep? Which lamb? Which ram? He replied
that God would decide. When they reached the
designated spot, the father prepared the fire and
tied the hands and feet of his son who'd fallen
asleep. His heart and his soul were heavy, but he
knew it was to ensure his prosperity. Strange.

Sacrificing his descendant to ensure his future. That's the way legends are. The father placed the son on the altar. He took the knife and raised his hand to slay his son, and then, one second, two seconds—

THE CHIEF:

That's enough!

SANDRO:

I haven't finished.

THE CHIEF:

You've been getting on my nerves ever since we boarded the ship.

SANDRO:

I haven't finished.

THE CHIEF:

When you're not babbling about suits and tailors, you're babbling about sheep and God. God's travelling with the rabble, two decks down, in tourist class. Leave him where he is.

SANDRO:

I haven't finished.

THE CHIEF:

Who told you that story?

SANDRO:

Somebody.

THE CHIEF:

Who?

THE DIPLOMAT enters.

THE DIPLOMAT:

I did. To console him.

THE BIOGRAPHER:

(*as he enters*) The lights went on in the smoking lounge. An animated group of fans rushed in, eager to hear The Chief tell more tales of his incredible exploits.

The lights go on. WILLY and JEREMY enter, followed by ALICE GENDRON, THE MINISTER and the three young ÉLISABETHS. The stewards serve THE CHIEF a whisky.

ALICE:

(*holding forth*) We've become a wealthy country by supplying others with the means to kill each other. Once the Nazis were defeated, we needed a new threat to ensure the survival of our war factories. After all, several eminent members of parliament own shares. Communism is the perfect pretext. Why do you think we've sent troops to Korea?

THE MINISTER:

Sometimes I miss life's ordinary moments, like: "Darling, I saw a necklace in the ship's gift shop."

Polite laughter. They sit down to play cards.

ALICE:

Would you like to play with us, Chief?

THE MINISTER:

I doubt the gentleman plays bridge.

ALICE:

How about poker then?

THE BIOGRAPHER:

The magic word!

ALICE:

Rumour has it you're a formidable player, Chief.

THE BIOGRAPHER:
    She knew how to chose her words.

THE MINISTER:
    (*Ignoring THE CHIEF.*) Bridge, Alice!

THE DIPLOMAT:
    Do you know how to play poker, Sandro?

SANDRO:
    Two pairs, three of a kind, full house, straight flush, four of a kind, royal flush.

THE MINISTER:
    Bridge!

SANDRO:
    (*to THE MINISTER*) We could play Black Jack, too.

THE MINISTER:
    Deal the cards, Alice.

    ALICE sits down beside THE CHIEF.

ALICE:
    How are our Italian friends, Chief?

THE MINISTER:
    You must be confusing this gentleman with some-one else.

ALICE:
    (*to THE CHIEF*) Do give them our regards. At least, the ones who aren't in jail. Lately we've been spending our days tearing pages out of our address books. We're going to miss their bribes.

SANDRO:
    What are "bribes?"

ALICE:
    Ask your father.

MARGUERITE enters the smoking lounge holding her sheet music.

THE MINISTER:
Were you rehearsing, dear?

ALICE:
That should make the Queen happy.

MARGUERITE:
What are you playing?

SANDRO:
We're playing at deciding what to play!

THE CHIEF:
(*chiding him*) Sandro!

SANDRO:
She's the one who's replacing my brother. What do they mean, she's got "connections."

ALICE:
This time, ask my husband.

THE MINISTER:
(*In an attempt to change the subject.*) So then, the three of you are named Élisabeth?

ÉLISABETH TURCOTTE:
Élisabeth Turcotte.

ÉLISABETH MÉNARD:
Élisabeth Ménard.

ÉLISABETH PENNINGTON:
Élisabeth Pennington.

THE MINISTER:
Alice, did you know all three young ladies were contest winners?

ÉLISABETH TURCOTTE:

>It was a contest organized for women named Elizabeth.

ÉLISABETH PENNINGTON:

>And born the same day as the Queen.

ÉLISABETH MÉNARD:

>There's twenty-one of us on the boat.

THE MINISTER:

>Twenty-one!

ÉLISABETH TURCOTTE:

>The others are in tourist class.

THE MINISTER:

>Oh, I see!

ÉLISABETH PENNINGTON:

>There was a contest within the contest. To choose three of the twenty-one to be in first class.

ÉLISABETH MÉNARD:

>Us three were upgraded.

ALICE:

>I can hear that at a glance! Black Jack, anyone?

THE DIPLOMAT:

>We have to set the stakes.

THE MINISTER:

>There are no stakes in bridge.

ÉLISABETH MÉNARD:

>Our purses and our shoes were supplied by Simpson-Sears.

ÉLISABETH TURCOTTE:

>And our gloves by Eaton's.

THE MINISTER:
　You've shuffled the cards enough, Alice.

MARGUERITE:
　(*to the stewards*) Tea, please.

THE CHIEF:
　Sandro, choose one of these nice young ladies and
　sit with her.

SANDRO:
　With the diplomat!

THE DIPLOMAT:
　He's the one who insists.

THE BIOGRAPHER:
　Sandro put his glasses back on.

SANDRO:
　(*as he puts his glasses on*) Please?

　　SANDRO sits beside THE DIPLOMAT.

THE MINISTER:
　There are too many of us for bridge. Two teams of
　two.

　　*Despite what THE BIOGRAPHER says, ALICE never
　　deals the cards which she shuffles continuously.*

THE BIOGRAPHER:
　A card game would follow. The minister's wife
　would win the first game. Full house of kings.

THE DIPLOMAT:
　(*to everyone*) Did you know that the lark is the
　symbol of man's yearning for joy?

THE BIOGRAPHER:
　Then it would be the diplomat's turn to take the
　pot, without even laying down his hand.

WILLY and JEREMY serve tea to the ladies and after-dinner drinks to the men.

WILLY:
Tea, Madam?

ALICE:
Cognac, like the gentlemen.

THE MINISTER:
Your medication, Alice. (*to the steward*) Madam wants tea.

ÉLISABETH MÉNARD:
Me, too.

ÉLISABETH TURCOTTE:
Me, too.

ÉLISABETH PENNINGTON:
Me, too.

ALICE:
Cognac!

JEREMY:
(*to the ÉLISABETHS*) Cream? Sugar?

ÉLISABETH TURCOTTE:
Me, too.

ÉLISABETH PENNINGTON:
Me, too.

ÉLISABETH MÉNARD:
Me, too.

THE CHIEF:
I'll have another whisky, please!

THE BIOGRAPHER:

The Chief would have a winning streak. He'd win three games in a row.

MADEMOISELLE LAVALLÉE enters, holding an enormous Indian headdress.

ALICE:

Do you have another surprise for us, Mademoiselle Lavallée?

MADEMOISELLE LAVALLÉE:

I asked him to wear his headdress. Just for tonight. He refuses. They all refuse. I told them how happy it would make us. I told them there are Belgians on board, along with the French and even the British passengers, it would make such a nice story for them to take home. But, no. They refuse to cooperate.

She exits.

ÉLISABETH PENNINGTON:

What I really, really like in first class is everybody's so polite.

ÉLISABETH MÉNARD:

Everybody says hello to you.

ÉLISABETH PENNINGTON:

Everybody uses such fancy words.

ALICE:

We never know who we might need tomorrow.

ÉLISABETH MÉNARD:

They say first class is really expensive.

ALICE:

I wouldn't know. We're subsidized!

THE MINISTER:
The cards, Alice!

THE DIPLOMAT:
So, when are they calling the election?

ALICE:
The Prime Minister intends to ruin our summer.
I can see myself already, sweating in some
godforsaken backwater, attending some wedding
celebration, sitting in a horse-drawn wagon, waving
bye-bye to the local farmers. What torture! I can see
myself visiting people on their death bed in the
hospitals, trying to get their vote before the doctors
get their souls. I loathe sick people, they always
look so ... sick.

THE DIPLOMAT:
There are rumours it will be in August.

ALICE:
The tenth!

THE MINISTER:
(*exploding*) Alice!

MARGUERITE:
Mama!

ALICE:
The election will be held the 10th of August.

THE MINISTER:
Alice and dates! I'm the only one who ever
remembers our wedding anniversary!

ALICE:
This is a ploy to make me shut up.

THE MINISTER:

Would you rather have me simply tell you to shut up?

Embarrassed silence. ALICE shuffles the cards energetically.

ALICE:

Shut up? That's all I've done since we entered politics. I was dumb enough to believe that it was a field for people with opinions.

MARGUERITE:

(*hoping to escape*) You'll have to excuse me—

ALICE GENDRON:

Stay here! I want you to see how your mother honours her responsibilities.

ÉLISABETH MÉNARD:

(*glancing at THE DIPLOMAT*) There's lots of handsome bachelors in first class.

ALICE:

If he's good-looking, you'll end up in one of his brothels. If he's well-spoken, you'll end up the wife of a minister.

ÉLISABETH PENNINGTON:

I'd love that!

ALICE:

Love what? Whore or wife of a minister?

ÉLISABETH PENNINGTON:

Wife of a minister!

ALICE:

Learning to hold your handbag, a bouquet of flowers and the programme for the day all in one hand, for hours on end, without getting paralysed? Yawning elegantly during the receptions? Sleeping with your eyes open during the speeches? Spending your days with a dumb smile on your face? Becoming addicted to tea sandwiches? Looking touched by the pimply cadets who present you with stuffed wild life? Swallowing, without making a face, an Eskimo soup of seal meat in whale blubber bouillon, or strips of cured buffalo from the Canadian Prairies? Does all that interest you? Dressing Ottawa-style? Does that really interest you?

ÉLISABETH PENNINGTON:
Well ...

ALICE:
Feeling ashamed to be rich in poverty-stricken neighbourhoods? Holding back your tears in the orphanages?

THE MINISTER:
Alice!

ALICE:
(*gravely*) Sizing up others, learning to quickly recognize their rank in life? Taking sides, in a single glance, with people you hate and ignoring the ones you like? Knowing how to use at the right moment words that can hurt or inspire fear? Enjoying the company of the backroom dealers in your riding, peddling political favours. Dining with the local mafia?

THE MINISTER:
Come with me.

ALICE:

Mastering the latest demagogic jargon, sniffing out the money to be made, spreading rumours? Scheming and plotting? Using the loopholes of a law to protect your own interests? Does that really interest you, young lady? You'll start speaking the language of official slogans, the language that masks the historical controversies.

MARGUERITE:

I'm afraid you'll have to excuse us.

ALICE:

Why? The game just started.

THE MINISTER:

Make an effort, Alice.

ALICE:

(*throwing the cards on the floor*) For years now, Joseph, you've had at your side the living proof of what a woman can accomplish by making an effort. It's an effort for me to get up in the morning, an effort to go to bed at night. Every time I push the wheelchair with what remains of our son, every time I bathe him, every time I feed him, I'm making an effort, a patriotic effort. I make the effort of trying to forget! Of trying to follow your party's doctrine. Coast-to-coast amnesia! Your government has raised the faculty of forgetting to the rank of a national value. Your government has succeeded in making us believe that the Dieppe massacre never existed, that it was simply a dress rehearsal for a future landing. There are one thousand two hundred Canadian mothers who gave birth to extras for a dress rehearsal. Our sons didn't really die—they were just rehearsing!

THE MINISTER:

That was eleven years ago.

ALICE:

Eleven years that I've been remembering the
British commanders' big blunder. Eleven years
that you've been forgetting. It was supposed to be
nighttime, it was broad daylight.

THE MINISTER:

Our sons are heroes.

ALICE:

It was supposed to be foggy, the sun was shining.

THE MINISTER:

They fought for the greater good of the world.

ALICE:

The beach was supposed to be sandy, it was rocky.

THE MINISTER:

They didn't hide in churchtowers, or in a wedding
race marrying the first girl who came along, nor
did they hide behind the speeches of the
nationalists.

ALICE:

Do you know how my sons rehearsed their death?
They were in their boat along with six hundred
other French Canadians, waiting for the order to
land. Meanwhile on the beach, the boys from
Ontario, Manitoba, Nova Scotia were already
spilling their blood.

THE DIPLOMAT:

Up on the cliffs, the Germans dominated everything.

ALICE:

By some miracle, a dozen men from Ontario
managed to get across the beach and into town. As
soon as they found shelter, they sent a short radio
message to headquarters to announce their feat.
But—

THE DIPLOMAT:

The radio transmission was jammed for a second or
two.

ALICE:

One second, two seconds.

THE DIPLOMAT:

One word ...

ALICE:

Two words.

THE DIPLOMAT:

Headquarters misunderstood. Headquarters
understood that the entire Ontario regiment had
entered Dieppe. Headquarters thought the landing
was a success.

ALICE:

And then ... the French Canadians received their
orders to land.

THE DIPLOMAT:

(*with emotion*) Between seven and seven-fifteen
in the morning, within fifteen minutes, hundreds
of young men ... Anything that moved on the
beach ... The Germans even shot at the corpses,
as if they wanted to kill us twice.

ALICE:

The ones I loved, the ones I loved ...

THE MINISTER:

Learn to forget!

ALICE:

I gave birth to Pierre, Paul and Arthur to help
Mackenzie King, who wanted to help Churchill who
wanted to help Stalin. Stalin who had already
helped Hitler, Stalin who today no longer helps
anyone.

THE MINISTER:

All these things in your head ... If only you could
forget, darling.

ALICE:

The following morning in London, the headlines
reported the handful of wounded British soldiers,
but not one word about the hundreds of Canadians
who had died. No protest was issued from Ottawa.
Hardly surprising from a country that still acts like
a colony. Banknotes, stamps, parliament, the
legislative system, all in the image of the imperialist
monarchs.

THE MINISTER:

Come take your tranquilizers. Come!

ALICE:

We have a big house, a beautiful garden. We know
how to drink tea and play bridge. And that's what
counts.

THE MINISTER:

I'm afraid you'll have to excuse us.

ALICE:

Tomorrow you'll see. I'll laugh and joke again.
Tomorrow ... Sometimes, when the medication fails

to bury the memories, I can hear, deep inside me, a rousing "Long live anarchy."

ALICE exits. MARGUERITE gathers up the cards.

THE MINISTER:
She's a rebel. When she was younger, she knew how to control herself. Since the boys' death ... alcohol ... and the medication ... She confuses rumours and official versions. At night she says our sons come to haunt her ... I don't want to know. I don't need to know. I need to sleep. She's a rebel. That's why I've always loved her. Good night. (*He exits. Beat. He returns.*) I hope I can count on your discretion about the election date.

He exits.

MARGUERITE:
I'm terribly sorry about all this. Really.

There is a moment of awkward silence. Everyone is lost in his or her own thoughts.

THE BIOGRAPHER:
The Chief had withdrawn and was counting his winnings. The Diplomat was bursting with pride over his military exploits. The young pianist could already hear the bravos that would follow her concert. Sandro and the young Élisabeths were flirting innocently. An atmosphere of gaiety reigned in the main lounge.

SANDRO:
(*taking THE DIPLOMAT's hand*) You must have suffered a lot, Jerome?

THE DIPLOMAT:

(*distressed by his memories*) Eleven hours on the beach in Dieppe. Thirty-four months in the Nazi prison camps.

ÉLISABETH MÉNARD:

Sambas, cha-chas. There's gonna be an orchestra tonight in tourist class.

ÉLISABETH TURCOTTE:

In tourist class?

ÉLISABETH PENNINGTON:

We can't change classes like that.

THE DIPLOMAT:

(*sombre*) The Germans tied us together in groups of ten, for two months, we had to pull down the pants of the man beside us so he could satisfy his most elementary needs.

ALL THREE ÉLISABETHS:

Okay! Let's go!

They exit.

THE CHIEF:

Sandro, it's time for you to go to bed.

THE DIPLOMAT:

(*to SANDRO*) Tomorrow at four, at the tailor's.

SANDRO:

Tomorrow at four.

THE CHIEF:

You don't have permission.

SANDRO:

Buonasera. (*He exits.*)

THE DIPLOMAT:

> *Buonasera*, Sandro. Just as the father was about to slay his son … One second, two seconds … An angel stayed his hand. God promised him great prosperity. The father was named Abraham, the son, Isaac … (*nodding to the gathering*) Good night, Mademoiselle, Messieurs.

> *THE DIPLOMAT exits.*

MARGUERITE:

> (*to THE CHIEF, intimidated*) Perhaps this isn't the right moment, but I wanted to tell you that your son is a great pianist and you shouldn't leave him alone like that on the deck. He might do something rash.

THE CHIEF:

> I haven't dared take a walk on the deck since the ship left Montreal. He's been posted there like a living reminder of my mistakes.

MARGUERITE:

> I think it's because of the arthritis that's affected his hands—

THE CHIEF:

> Arthritis? What arthritis? Someone crushed his hands. A misunderstanding.

MARGUERITE:

> (*horrified*) I didn't realize.

THE CHIEF:

> It's been a while since I've terrorized anyone. It feels good. You go tell him to come in.

MARGUERITE:

> Me?

THE CHIEF:

I want to get some fresh air without bumping into him.

MARGUERITE:

I wouldn't know what to say to him.

THE CHIEF:

Tell him I've found a solution for our passports.

THE BIOGRAPHER:

A solution?

THE CHIEF:

Tell him I have our passports. He'll come in.

MARGUERITE:

Good night! (*She exits.*)

THE BIOGRAPHER:

What is your solution?

THE CHIEF:

You're the author. Find one!

> *THE CHIEF sinks into his armchair.*

Part Two

Episode 5

*On the deck, the same evening. Fog. MARGUERITE
joins ÉTIENNE. The foghorn sounds every thirty
seconds.*

MARGUERITE:

You should come inside.

ÉTIENNE:

What about my happiness? When are you going to
make me happy? I waited for you all day yesterday,
all night and all day today. I stayed here, without
moving. I stayed here so you wouldn't have to go
looking for me. I've waited for you in the cold,
without eating, all this time. I turned around
hundreds of times, thinking I heard you breathing.
And where I thought I felt your presence I saw
shapes in the mist beckoning me to follow. At dusk,
the flames on the horizon were dancing around my
head. Then with darkness came the chimera. The
sea lent them haunting voices. "Jump, jump into
the void." To escape the hallucinations, I should
have jumped into the void. You were the only one
who could stop me. The only one to bring comfort.
I jumped ten, twenty times and you weren't there
to hold me back. Nothing! What were you doing all
this time?

MARGUERITE:

> I was rehearsing.

ÉTIENNE:

> I've spent all this time reviewing my life, erasing
> everything that could make me want to cling to it. I
> expected some consideration from you, if only out
> of gratitude for the moment of musical pleasure I
> once gave you. I even thought that pity would
> provide you with a pretext for some concern. But,
> no. Nothing! You were thinking about your future!

MARGUERITE:

> Yes.

ÉTIENNE:

> You were betraying me with Chopin!

MARGUERITE:

> That's right.

ÉTIENNE:

> I'm very disappointed in you.

MARGUERITE:

> To throw themselves into the void, some people
> choose to play with colours, others with words, or
> movement. You and I have music. Music can
> console you. Not the music you used to have in
> your hands, but the music that is still inside you.
> Come. We'll stop by the kitchen and order you a
> hot meal. Afterwards, we'll play cards with the
> others. I'll hold your cards for you.

ÉTIENNE:

> Really, your tact is overwhelming!

MARGUERITE:

> And then you'll make me rehearse till dawn.

ÉTIENNE:
Leave me alone.

Beat.

MARGUERITE:
You can also forgive him.

ÉTIENNE:
Forgive who?

MARGUERITE:
Your father.

ÉTIENNE:
Forgive! Add humiliation to outrage?

MARGUERITE:
Then you will stop punishing yourself.

ÉTIENNE:
What do you know about me? What do you know?

MARGUERITE:
I know he's the cause of your accident.

ÉTIENNE:
Is he the one who sent you? Really, money can buy anything.

MARGUERITE:
He told me to tell you that he has your passports.

ÉTIENNE:
What?

MARGUERITE:
He told me he found a solution for your passports.

ÉTIENNE:
A solution? And I'm supposed to believe him? Why should I believe him now?

MARGUERITE:

He also told me about your hands.

ÉTIENNE:

(*surprised*) He really told you about my hands?

MARGUERITE:

Yes ... and he seemed sad.

ÉTIENNE:

Him sad? And he seemed sincere?

MARGUERITE:

Forgive him!

ÉTIENNE:

That's absurd!

MARGUERITE:

I've always believed in forgiveness. It allows us to ease our own pain and finally see the suffering of others.

ÉTIENNE:

(*violently*) Do you expect that kind of idiotic thinking to help you play Chopin? Chopin doesn't forgive. Chopin suffers!

MARGUERITE:

So stop being cynical and suffer! I want tears. I want cries. I want your whining to touch me. Arouse my pity. It is my pity you're after? I'm waiting. Go ahead! Use your legendary talent. Nothing? Nothing. How selfish. (*Beat.*) Victims are vicious. Suffering is their only weapon. Constantly repeating: look what they did to me. Look! Look! And that gives them the right to do anything. They become tyrants. They rule through resentment. They build countries on the fault of others. They are martyrs, gods, infinite, and we become their slaves. Whenever we glance at their sad eyes, we drown in their tears. Whenever we touch their wounds, scars form, holding our hands prisoner. I have a brother who lost all his limbs, a mother who lost two sons, a father who lost his illusions. They've taught me the gamut of deep sighs and heavy silences. In this field, you are a rank amateur. You should stop abusing people who care about you. Good night! (*She turns to leave.*)

ÉTIENNE:

Wait !

MARGUERITE:

I won't come back, Étienne.

ÉTIENNE:

(*sincere*) I'm making you play a cruel game. Forgive me. You see, I understand forgiveness. (*She looks at him.*) The first thing to remember: Chopin was one of the first to let the soloist take the spotlight. The orchestra simply reinforces the soloist's melody. Are you ready? We're going to play the concerto.

MARGUERITE:

There's a piano in the smoking lounge.

ÉTIENNE:

No, right here. Tell me. Go ahead. In the beginning ...

MARGUERITE:

In the beginning, there are the violins.

ÉTIENNE:

Tell me better than that.

We hear the second movement of Chopin's "Piano Concerto No. 1."

MARGUERITE:

In the beginning, the strings call to the piano.

ÉTIENNE:

What do you see?

MARGUERITE:

I see the orchestra.

ÉTIENNE:

No. What does this music inspire in you? What does it make you see?

MARGUERITE:

There's a woman. (*Beat.*) She's alone.

ÉTIENNE:

What else.

MARGUERITE:

Her back is turned to us.

    Beat.

ÉTIENNE:

Now the setting.

MARGUERITE:

Everything around her is arid.

    Beat.

ÉTIENNE:

What is she doing?

MARGUERITE:

She's waiting.

ÉTIENNE:

Romanze, larghetto.

MARGUERITE:

She's waiting for someone.

ÉTIENNE:

Let yourself feel the images.

MARGUERITE:

A silhouette appears before her.

ÉTIENNE:

What is it? Who is it? (*They look at each other.*) Now, put your hands on the keyboard.

> *Beat.*

MARGUERITE:

Then, we hear the breath of the entire orchestra spying on them in silence.

ÉTIENNE:

It's a first love that inspired the adagios of both concertos. (*Beat.*) I gave my first recital when I was eleven.

THE CHIEF:

(*in the Empress Lounge where he is sitting with* THE BIOGRAPHER) I'd invited all of Montreal's high society. It was the first time I heard him play. He was possessed by something beyond my grasp.

ÉTIENNE:

At the end of the first movement, just before resuming, I heard someone clap and yell "Bravo, bravo!"

THE CHIEF:

(*in the Empress Lounge*) "Bravo! Bravo!"

MARGUERITE:

Your father clapped between movements?

THE CHIEF:

(*in the Empress Lounge*) Later I found out it wasn't done.

MARGUERITE:

You must have been embarrassed?

ÉTIENNE:

He was so proud.

THE CHIEF:

(*in the Empress Lounge*) The entire audience started to clap with me.

MARGUERITE:

The entire audience?

THE CHIEF:

(*in the Empress Lounge*) They had no choice.

ÉTIENNE:

He did the same thing between every movement.

THE CHIEF:

(*in the Empress Lounge*) I want that to be written in the book.

MARGUERITE:

They still talk about you at the Conservatory. They say Chopin would have been moved to hear you play.

ÉTIENNE:

He has heard me play. *(They look at each other without saying a word.)* Marguerite ... It is "Marguerite"?

MARGUERITE:

Yes.

ÉTIENNE:

Marguerite … do you think a woman could still be interested in me?

MARGUERITE:

Yes. Come … A hot meal …

ÉTIENNE:

A woman! Not a nurse!

MARGUERITE:

Beauty comes from within.

ÉTIENNE:

Girl scout!

MARGUERITE:

Make my victory yours.

ÉTIENNE:

I couldn't even turn the pages of your music for you.

MARGUERITE:

I'm cold. (*He takes her in his arms.*) And now, the piano and the orchestra are one. She has found the one she was waiting for. Say something nice to me.

ÉTIENNE:

I think you're very beautiful.

MARGUERITE:

Do you want to take off your gloves?

He removes one glove.

ÉTIENNE:

You see, they've broken these three fingers three times in order to make them straight again, and here … (*She kisses his hand.*)

MARGUERITE:
> *Pianissimo.*

ÉTIENNE:
> I can't feel a thing.

MARGUERITE:
> Can we try your lips?

ÉTIENNE:
> We can try.

> *He kisses her with awkward, almost violent, passion.*

Empress Room.
SANDRO is being chased by JEREMY and WILLY.

WILLY:
Come back here! You cheated!

SANDRO:
I didn't cheat.

JEREMY:
You dropped two cards on the floor!

WILLY:
Give our money back!

SANDRO:
I won't!

JEREMY:
Give us our money!

SANDRO:
I won't.

> THE DIPLOMAT *enters, carrying a large box.*

THE DIPLOMAT:
What's going on?

WILLY:
We were playing poker and this young gentleman cheated, sir.

JEREMY:
With two hidden cards, sir.

SANDRO:

Only one. Don't listen to them.

THE DIPLOMAT:

I'm surprised to learn that the crew has permission
to play poker with the passengers.

JEREMY:

It's forbidden, sir.

WILLY:

But this young gentleman cheated, sir.

THE DIPLOMAT:

Perhaps we should forget the whole incident.

He offers them a generous tip. The stewards exit.

SANDRO:

I'd be dead if you hadn't shown up. (*THE DIPLOMAT
shows him the suit.*) My suit! *Magnifico! Splendido!* My
first real suit!

THE DIPLOMAT:

Do you like it?

SANDRO:

E'i piu' bel vestito della mia vita.

THE DIPLOMAT:

All the girls will fall for you!

SANDRO:

Tutte le ragazze!

THE DIPLOMAT:

They'll find you very handsome.

SANDRO:

Il piu'bello.

THE DIPLOMAT:
Feel how silky it is.

SANDRO strokes the suit.

SANDRO:
It's so silky.

THE DIPLOMAT:
They'll love the light glowing in your face.

THE DIPLOMAT furtively strokes SANDRO's face.

SANDRO:
No one has even shown so much interest in me. I want us to stay friends for life. Best friends. (*He goes to hug THE DIPLOMAT.*) Pass me the shirt. I'm going to try on my suit. (*SANDRO starts to get undressed.*) 338 crates of apples, oranges and other fruit. 24,430 pounds of flour. 9,000 pounds of sugar. 3,860 pounds of powdered milk … (*Beat.*) Why are you looking at me like that?

THE CHIEF and THE BIOGRAPHER enter. THE CHIEF sees SANDRO bare-chested. He seems strangely detached.

THE BIOGRAPHER:
Atlantic Ocean, latitude 50, longitude 266 west. The centre of the world. End of Day 3.

THE CHIEF:
Last night I woke up. In a cold sweat. The ship was in total silence, as if the engines had been cut. I thought the ship must have hit something, that the water was rising right below us. I thought, soon people will start screaming. The sirens will tell us to evacuate. The lights will go out and in the darkness of the ocean … I was suffocating in my bed! I told

101

myself: "Get up, go get your sons. They're all you have left. Your only fortune. Open the door to every cabin until you find them." Then I saw myself getting up and looking for my sons. I opened door after door. Dozens, hundreds of doors. And out of every cabin dead bodies came floating, face down, on a wave of icy water. I turned them over. It was never Étienne. Never Sandro. I was walking through the icy water, but I didn't feel the cold. My hands were slashed by broken glass, but I didn't feel my cuts. And I kept yelling: "I can't feel anything, I can't feel anything. I want to feel something. Anything. I can't feel anything." I was suffocating in my bed. That's when I got up for real. I left my cabin and came here. Everything was calm. The cleaning staff were working. They stopped and stared at me. In their eyes, I could see my own terror. I could see my trembling hands.

SANDRO:
See my new suit?

THE CHIEF:
And that's when I remembered that people had always respected me, always feared me, because I never felt anything. And that I should keep up the good habit.

SANDRO:
You see my new suit?

THE BIOGRAPHER:
The Diplomat opened one of the portholes.

THE DIPLOMAT:
(*stroking SANDRO's suit*) Are you going to take these passports...

THE BIOGRAPHER:
    One second.

THE DIPLOMAT:
    … Or should I feed them to the gulls?

THE BIOGRAPHER:
    Two seconds.

THE CHIEF:
    Give them to me!

THE DIPLOMAT:
    Sandro, go to my cabin.

SANDRO:
    I need my father's permission.

THE CHIEF:
    Go, Sandro. Go, go to his cabin.

SANDRO:
    You're the best father in the world.

    SANDRO exits.

THE DIPLOMAT:
    (*handing him the passports*) Here's the one for James.
    And one for Martin.

THE CHIEF:
    What about mine?

THE DIPLOMAT:
    Sandro will give you yours tomorrow morning, at
    daybreak.

THE CHIEF:
    Louise. She has long, blonde hair.

THE DIPLOMAT:
And hazel eyes. I already know a lot more about her than you do.

THE CHIEF:
(*to THE DIPLOMAT*) Make him drink.

THE DIPLOMAT:
Pardon me?

THE CHIEF:
Make him drunk first. Please.

THE DIPLOMAT:
You just saved their lives. That's worthy of a good father.

THE CHIEF:
Shut up.

THE DIPLOMAT:
His soul will be a bit heavier, but a soul without life just becomes another white cross in a field of white crosses. (*withdrawing*) Gentlemen.

He exits.
Foghorn.

THE BIOGRAPHER:
Excuse me, sir. I'm going to finish your biography.

THE CHIEF:
Should I order a bottle of whisky for the two of us?

THE BIOGRAPHER:
I don't need you any more.

THE CHIEF:
It's my life!

THE BIOGRAPHER:

We've gone so far into fiction, reality is of no use now. I'm going to finish it alone.

THE CHIEF:

How will it end?

THE BIOGRAPHER:

"The King of Darkness fell into the sea."

THE CHIEF:

I don't like that.

THE BIOGRAPHER:

"It was during a fierce fight with a diplomat who wanted to abuse his son that the King of Darkness fell into the sea."

THE CHIEF:

I don't like that.

ÉTIENNE enters. A bit tipsy. Radiant.

ÉTIENNE:

(*to* THE BIOGRAPHER) Well, if it isn't my father's author and his subject. If you can reinvent his life, reinvent mine! (*Lighthearted, he hums a cha-cha tune.*) Try!

THE BIOGRAPHER:

I work for your father, not you.

ÉTIENNE:

Write that I forgave my father. Write how, after much soul-searching, I managed to forget everything. Invent the circumstances. Invent that I was magnanimous. Give the details. Write the unimaginable.

THE BIOGRAPHER:

A story of forgiveness?

THE CHIEF:

Try!

THE BIOGRAPHER:

(*trying to find lines for them*) Alcohol had made the son vulnerable. Fatigue had made the father conciliatory. Enemies, by blood, they were about to play a game of reconciliation.

ÉTIENNE:

Go on.

THE BIOGRAPHER:

The father avoided the son's stare.

ÉTIENNE:

You should get some sleep.

    Beat.

THE BIOGRAPHER:

The son approached the father.

THE CHIEF:

I was on my way out.

THE BIOGRAPHER:

They finally looked each other in the eye.

ÉTIENNE:

Out? Where were you going?

THE BIOGRAPHER:

A moment of affection.

THE CHIEF:

I was worried about you.

ÉTIENNE:

About me?

THE BIOGRAPHER:

Dawn was breaking on the distant horizon, bringing the hope of better days. (*He exits.*)

ÉTIENNE:

I was dancing.

THE CHIEF:

You were dancing?

ÉTIENNE:

Strange, eh?

THE CHIEF:

Since when do you know how to dance?

ÉTIENNE:

Since this evening. Can I have a drink with you? My head is spinning. I like it. I'm not used to all this.

THE CHIEF:

Dancing, alcohol! We'll make a man of you yet.

ÉTIENNE:

After our dance, we found a piano. She's a pianist. She played. A bit pedestrian, but pleasant enough. She said I'd make a good teacher.

THE CHIEF:

You're chattering like a schoolgirl. Is she pretty?

ÉTIENNE:

Yes.

THE CHIEF:

Good, I have to get going.

ÉTIENNE:

Where?

THE CHIEF:
Eh?

ÉTIENNE:
Where are you going? Is everything okay, Papa? You look worried.

THE CHIEF:
I've got your new passport. (*He hands it to him.*) Put it somewhere safe.

ÉTIENNE:
Did it all go smoothly?

THE CHIEF:
As usual. As usual. (*Beat.*) So, you went dancing?

ÉTIENNE:
Yes. Latin American dances.

THE CHIEF:
You say she's pretty?

ÉTIENNE:
Yes.

THE CHIEF:
You didn't promise her anything?

ÉTIENNE:
No.

THE CHIEF:
Never promise women anything. Don't forget, when we reach London, we're going to disappear.

ÉTIENNE:
I haven't forgotten. (*reading his passport*) "James Peacock."

THE CHIEF:
Put you passport somewhere safe.

ÉTIENNE:

Yes.

THE CHIEF:

I'm going for a walk.

ÉTIENNE:

Put a coat on.

THE CHIEF:

What?

ÉTIENNE:

It's getting cooler. (*They look at each other in silence.*)
We'll try to be happy over there.

THE CHIEF:

Yes.

ÉTIENNE:

We'll get a fresh start?

THE CHIEF:

That's right.

ÉTIENNE.

New names. New lives.

THE CHIEF:

Your passport is your most precious possession.

ÉTIENNE:

We'll forgive everything and forget.

THE CHIEF:

No, Étienne. (*Beat.*) Never forgive anybody.
Especially those who have no regrets. No regrets,
no forgiveness! The longer you withhold your
forgiveness, the longer you maintain your authority.
Forgiveness granted, respect lost.

ÉTIENNE:

I forgive you for my hands, Papa.

THE CHIEF:

They didn't hit you on the head, did they?! How can you forgive me? I thought you had more pride than that! No regrets, no forgiveness. There's no such thing as regret. There's destiny. That's all. There are winners, and losers. The powerful and the underdogs. Pretending there are nuances is what life is all about.

ÉTIENNE:

I don't want to spend my life hating you.

THE CHIEF:

Your destiny, Étienne, is to hate me. Fathers and sons are made to hate each other. We hate each other, we betray each other, we judge each other, we ignore each other, but we never forgive anything. You'll see. Your sons won't give a damn about everything you did for them.

ÉTIENNE:

Does it have to be that way?

THE CHIEF:

I promised you a new life, not a new father! Look at the lines on my face, Étienne! There must be one or two that tell you I'm despicable.

ÉTIENNE:

I want to see something else.

THE CHIEF:

Stop!

ÉTIENNE:

I forgive you!

THE CHIEF:

Stop! I gave Sandro to the diplomat. Isn't that enough to make you take back your forgiveness?

ÉTIENNE:

She told me you found a solution.

THE CHIEF:

I sacrificed Sandro to save our lives. That was the only solution. I had to do it, but it's despicable.

ÉTIENNE:

What's the diplomat's cabin number?

THE CHIEF:

Take back your forgiveness!

ÉTIENNE:

What's his cabin number?

THE CHIEF:

Take back your forgiveness!

ÉTIENNE:

(*He exits, shouting.*) Sandro! Sandro!

The Empress Lounge.
Jeremy is standing beside a record player. There's a
chair in the middle of the room. The passengers are all
dressed in their fancy Coronation ceremony clothes.
The women are wearing tiaras and The Minister is
wearing a tuxedo.

MADEMOISELLE LAVALLÉE:

(*equipped with a megaphone*) The Queen will stand
beside the simple Coronation chair that is six
hundred and fifty years old. The Marquess of
Salisbury will step forward with the Sovereign's
Sword. The Archbishop of Canterbury will pass it to
the Queen. Then they'll bring the glittering Orb.
The Archbishop will then raise Saint Edward's
crown and place it on the Queen's head. At that
point, all the guests will say: "God save the Queen!"
Then there'll be the procession. As soon as the
Queen approaches, look dignified. It's easy. She
inspires respect. When she passes in front of you,
you must pay your respects. The men?

THE MINISTER:
We bow our heads.

MADEMOISELLE LAVALLÉE:
And the women?

WOMEN:
We take the hand of the gentleman standing next
to us. We lift the hem of our skirt, brace ourselves

on one leg, bend our knee, bow our head, keep
our eyes lowered ...

ALICE:

And if we could fall through the floor, we would.

ÉLISABETH PENNINGTON:

What if she doesn't walk by? Then whatta we
supposed to do?

ALICE:

My dear, every time you open your mouth, I feel as
if we're back in *la belle province.*

MADEMOISELLE LAVALLÉE:

Don't worry. Somebody's bound to walk by you, a
Prince Philip or a Princess Margaret.

ÉLISABETH PENNINGTON:

Or a Queen Mother.

ÉLISABETH TURCOTTE:

Or a Prince Charles.

ÉLISABETH MÉNARD:

A Princess Anne.

ÉLISABETH PENNINGTON:

A Princess Marina.

MADEMOISELLE LAVALLÉE:

A Princess Alexandra.

ÉLISABETH MÉNARD:

A Duke of Kent.

ÉLISABETH TURCOTTE:

A Duchess of Kent.

ALICE:

Anyway, the remains of something we're supposed
to bow to.

MARGUERITE enters.

MARGUERITE:
Sorry, I was rehearsing.

ALICE:
So are we.

THE MINISTER:
So! When do we eat?

MADEMOISELLE LAVALLÉE:
You can go for breakfast when the rehearsal is over.

THE MINISTER:
What are we waiting for?

MADEMOISELLE LAVALLÉE:
The end of the rehearsal.

THE MINISTER:
We've already rehearsed the whole thing twice. The bows, the entire ceremony!

ALICE:
If the royal family falls ill, we'll be able to replace them! Mademoiselle Lavallée?

MADEMOISELLE LAVALLÉE:
Yes, Madame Gendron?

ALICE:
Are we marking time?

MADEMOISELLE LAVALLÉE:
The Indians are putting on their costumes and— they refuse to collaborate.

THE MINISTER:
This is ridiculous!

MADEMOISELLE LAVALLÉE:
  We'll go through it once more. In case they decide
  to come. Mademoiselle Gendron, you can play the
  Queen.

ÉLISABETH MÉNARD:
  Lucky you!

MARGUERITE:
  I don't know—

THE MINISTER:
  Yes, you know!

ÉLISABETH TURCOTTE:
  They say the Queen's makeup has to be perfect.

ÉLISABETH MÉNARD:
  It has to go with the yellow lighting in Westminster
  Abbey.

ÉLISABETH PENNINGTON:
  And the pinks lights on her coach.

ÉLISABETH TURCOTTE:
  It has to be bright enough for the black and white
  photographs.

MADEMOISELLE LAVALLÉE:
  But not too bright for the colour photos.

THE MINISTER:
  Can we get this over with?

ÉLISABETH TURCOTTE:
  Don't forget the television cameras and the movies.

MADEMOISELLE LAVALLÉE:
  They even did all sorts of tests with a young girl.

ÉLISABETH MÉNARD:
  They say her skin is just like the Queen's.

ÉLISABETH PENNINGTON:
The same shape face.

ÉLISABETH MÉNARD:
Let's face it, that girl hit the jackpot!

ÉLISABETH TURCOTTE:
The jackpot for sure!

THE MINISTER:
I'm going to have breakfast!

ALICE:
(*laughing*) Such impatience, Joseph!

MADEMOISELLE LAVALLÉE:
Now, Mademoiselle Gendron, play the Queen for
us.

MARGUERITE:
What am I supposed to do?

MADEMOISELLE LAVALLÉE:
The Queen will stand beside the simple Coronation
chair that is six hundred and fifty years old. The
Marquess of Salisbury will step forward...

THE MINISTER:
(*exasperated*) Go over to that chair, put that thing on
your head and walk by us.

MADEMOISELLE LAVALLÉE:
This time, Mr. Minister, you're going to play the
Archbishop.

THE MINISTER:
The pope, if it will speed things up!

MADEMOISELLE LAVALLÉE:
The Anglicans don't have a pope—

THE MINISTER:
(*increasingly impatient*) IT WAS A JOKE, MADEMOISELLE LAVALLÉE! A JOKE!

ALICE:
(*laughing*) Joseph!

THE MINISTER:
I'M HUNGRY!

MADEMOISELLE LAVALLÉE:
(*into the megaphone*) Everyone ready!

ALL TOGETHER:
Yes!

MADEMOISELLE LAVALLÉE:
Good, we can begin. It's going to be wonderful. All set?

ALL TOGETHER:
Yes.

MADEMOISELLE LAVALLÉE:
Let's go! Willy, start the music!

JEREMY:
I'm Jeremy, madam.

THE MINISTER:
Jeremy, start the music!

JEREMY:
Yes, sir!

JEREMY plays "God Save the Queen."

MADEMOISELLE LAVALLÉE:
(*into the megaphone*) Go ahead, Mr. Minister. (*THE MINISTER places the substitute crown on MARGUERITE's head.*) God Save the Queen!

ALL TOGETHER (*except ALICE*):
God save the Queen!

MADEMOISELLE LAVALLÉE:
(*into the megaphone*) You make a very touching
queen, Mademoiselle Gendron.

ÉLISABETH TURCOTTE:
It's true, you make a beautiful queen.

MADEMOISELLE LAVALLÉE:
(*into the megaphone*) You don't speak to the Queen
unless she speaks to you!

THE MINISTER:
Let's keep going.

MADEMOISELLE LAVALLÉE:
(*into the megaphone*) Now, the three Élisabeths. Your
hand, your dress, your knee, your eyes. Perfect. You
look as if you've been doing this all your life.
(*MARGUERITE walks by the passengers.*) Now the bows,
Mr. Minister. Perfect! A professional bower!

THE MINISTER:
We can do without your comments, Mademoiselle
Lavallée.

MADEMOISELLE LAVALLÉE:
It was a joke, Mr. Minister. Your turn, Madame
Gendron! Go ahead, your hand … Your hand,
Madame Gendron.

THE MINISTER:
Your hand, Alice!

MADEMOISELLE LAVALLÉE:
(*into the megaphone, ALICE isn't moving*) Madame
Gendron! It's your turn! Bow to the Queen!

ALICE:

No, she's my daughter!

MADEMOISELLE LAVALLÉE:

(*into the megaphone*) Yes, but she's playing the Queen.

ALICE:

Yes, but she's my daughter.

MADEMOISELLE LAVALLÉE:

Jeremy, stop the music!

JEREMY:

Yes, madam.

JEREMY stops the music.

THE MINISTER:

Now what's the matter?

ALICE:

I don't want our daughter to be the Queen of England.

THE MINISTER:

Alice!!! How far do you intend to take the ridiculous this morning?

ALICE:

I admit it would be hard to go much farther. We've already turned a masquerade party into a perfect farce.

THE MINISTER:

Alice! In my entire career, there hasn't been a single member of the Opposition who's put me through the paces like you've put me through the paces in the four days since we left Montreal. Alice, you've taken more energy out of me than an election campaign. Alice! Alice! Alice! I must have exhausted the patience of all the other passengers repeating your name.

MADEMOISELLE LAVALLÉE:
Now let's start over.

THE MINISTER:
I'm talking to my wife!

MADEMOISELLE LAVALLÉE:
You have certain obligations, Mr. Minister!

THE MINISTER:
Let's talk about my obligations! My friends inquire about the Prime Minister's health before inquiring about my own. To stay in office, I'm constantly getting bogged down in compromises that go against the French Canadians' hard-won rights. My government is about to assert our autonomy from England so we can be free to sell the country to the Americans. I pretend to like everyone when I hate almost everyone!

ALICE:
Am I one of the people you hate, Joseph?

THE MINISTER:
(*touched*) You? (*Beat.*) You, who dares say aloud the words that haunt me; you, who have born the insomnia, the grief, the loss of my sons; you, who have made the effort to love me in spite of all my contradictions; you, all that is left of my conscience ... Of all the truths I know, there is only one I have never been ashamed of: I love you, Alice.

MADEMOISELLE LAVALLÉE:
This is no place for this kind of thing!

MARGUERITE:
Mademoiselle Lavallée, go see whether you can make yourself useful somewhere else.

MADEMOISELLE LAVALLÉE:
I don't have to take orders from you.

ÉLISABETH MÉNARD:
She's the Queen!

ÉLISABETH TURCOTTE AND ÉLISABETH PENNINGTON:
It's true, she's the Queen!

MADEMOISELLE LAVALLÉE:
Fine! Very well! Perfect! (*into the megaphone*) Breakfast is served! (*She exits.*)

ÉLISABETH TURCOTTE:
We're going to have breakfast in tourist class.

ÉLISABETH MÉNARD:
I hope they have games like yesterday.

ÉLISABETH PENNINGTON:
No, let's stay in first class.

ÉLISABETH MÉNARD:
It's more fun in tourist class.

> *They exit with* MADEMOISELLE LAVALLÉE.

ALICE:
Are you going to join us, Marguerite? Your father has whetted my appetite!

THE MINISTER:
(*to his wife*) How would you like to prolong our trip and go to France after London?

ALICE:

What about the elections?

THE MINISTER:

They say that Italy is lovely in August.

ALICE:

Rome on the tenth?

THE MINISTER:

Rome on the tenth.

> *ÉTIENNE enters. He is wearing the same clothes as the previous day. He looks lost, exhausted. Deeply disturbed...*

THE MINISTER:

Are you coming, Marguerite?

ALICE:

Marguerite?

MARGUERITE:

(*distracted*) Yes, yes. (*THE MINISTER and his wife exit.*) I waited for you for my lesson.

ÉTIENNE:

Your lesson? There won't be any lessons.

MARGUERITE:

You have blood on your shirt!

ÉTIENNE:

I came to tell you that everything you said about forgiveness was idiotic. There's no sense in forgiving. It was stupid of me to listen to you. Because of you, I was humiliated like no one has ever been humiliated.

MARGUERITE:

Because of me?

122

ÉTIENNE:

There I was, facing him—

MARGUERITE:

Facing who?

ÉTIENNE:

For a split second, I was ready to rewrite history
with him. For a moment, I was his heir. Everything
was possible between us. For a moment, I was his
son. And that's when I forgave him. I turned my
cheek and he ... he struck me down. (*Ironically.*)
The crippled saint forgiving his tormentor. I mixed
up everything. My anger, your tenderness, his
ambition. When in fact, there was nothing but my
grief.

MARGUERITE:

(*going to embrace him*) Étienne!

ÉTIENNE:

(*turning away*) It was stupid of me to listen to you.

MARGUERITE:

(*upset*) I'm going to rehearse.

ÉTIENNE:

Rehearse what?

MARGUERITE:

We're approaching the coast of Ireland. There isn't
much time left before my concert.

ÉTIENNE:

Concert?

MARGUERITE:

Chopin.

ÉTIENNE:

> (*cynically*) Yes, go rehearse. You're right, I'm afraid you don't have enough time to come up with an even acceptable Chopin.

MARGUERITE:

> That's cruel!

ÉTIENNE:

> And what about you? You're not cruel? You're constantly talking to me about music—the one thing I have to forget. You despise victims, but when it comes to feeding off them—this is where your advice would be most judicious! A teenage girl desperate for emotion tells me to forgive and I listen to her. For a few kisses! A substitute on top of it all … My downfall truly has begun. My father was right about one thing: it's better to deal with whores. They don't expect anything from you except your money. (*Beat.*) You're hurt?! Try to forgive me now.

MARGUERITE:

> Yes, I'm hurt.

ÉTIENNE:

> Go on being hurt! Maybe it will help you understand Chopin!

> *She leaves.*

Episode 8

First-class deck.
Sunshine.
With Sandro *at his side,* The Chief, *his biography in his hand, is scanning the horizon.* Sandro *is wearing his new suit.*

Sandro:
> *24,430 libbre di farina. 9,000 libbre di zucchero.*

The Chief:
> Three more days and we'll be in Liverpool.

Sandro:
> *2,240 libbre di formaggio, 1,100 di cafe', 700 di the'.*

The Chief:
> You smell of booze! That was your first binge, eh?

Sandro:
> *22,150 libbre di carne di bue.*

The Chief:
> I'm going to teach you how to drink.

Sandro:
> *17,105 di carne de maiale.*

The Chief:
> Alcohol can make you lose your head. Until you can't even remember what you did. But afterwards, you forget everything. I'll teach you about women, too. Lots of women.

SANDRO:

> *4,125 libbre di pomodori.*

> *ÉTIENNE joins them.*

THE CHIEF:

> Good morning, James. (*Showing them his biography.*)
> Look at this, it's my life. It's grand, it's bigger and
> better. In this, I'm a good man. He wrote a happy
> ending for us. (*Reading.*) A few days after their
> arrival in London, the Chief and his sons
> inaugurated their new identities and attended the
> Coronation procession. Later that day they were
> seen at the Commonwealth Gala where Marguerite
> Gendron played a Chopin concerto full of sadness
> and pain. Several months later, Étienne married a
> pretty Irish girl. Sandro entered the military
> service.

ÉTIENNE:

> Happy ending.

SANDRO:

> *Bella fine.*

THE CHIEF:

> (*reading*) Elizabeth II's reign was long and
> prosperous and the French Canadians remained
> her faithful subjects. The End. What's your name,
> James? What is your name?

ÉTIENNE:

> My name is Mister James Peacock and I live in
> Gloucester, England.

THE CHIEF:

> Martin?

SANDRO:

My name is Martin and I live in Gloucester, England.

THE CHIEF:

Now, Martin, give me my passport. My passport, please.

> *THE CHIEF takes two dead larks out of SANDRO's pockets.*

THE CHIEF:

What's that?

SANDRO:

Allodole.

ÉTIENNE:

Larks. (*Beat.*) He's dead.

SANDRO:

Una secondo.

THE CHIEF:

Who's dead?

SANDRO:

Due secondi.

ÉTIENNE:

The diplomat!

THE CHIEF:

What happened?

ÉTIENNE:

He fell overboard. (*Beat.*) We helped him.

THE CHIEF:

Sandro, give me my passport. The passport the diplomat gave you.

SANDRO:

> He said he had something for you in his vest
> pocket, but he didn't have time to give it to me.

ÉTIENNE:

> No, he didn't have time.

SANDRO:

> *338 casse di mele, arance e altra frutta.*
>
> *Foghorn.*

THE BIOGRAPHER:

> (*reading*) Dear reader, How can a humble
> biography such as this possibly tell the life story of a
> man whose career was as exceptional as that of the
> Chief of Chiefs? His birth, alone, was an event the
> devil heralded with a total eclipse ...
>
> *The foghorn drowns his voice.*

THE END